Professional Coaching Competencies: The Complete Guide

Damian Goldvarg
Patricia A. Mathews
Norma Perel

Foreword by Jeffrey E. Auerbach

Executive College Press

Library of Congress Cataloging-in-Publication Data
Goldvarg, D., Mathews, N. A., & Perel, N.
Professional Coaching Competencies: The Complete Guide / Damian Goldvarg, Patricia A. Mathews & Norma Perel—1st ed.
p. cm.
Includes bibliographical references.

ISBN 978-1-5323-7682-5
Library of Congress Control Number: 2018945662

1. Personal Coaching
2. Executive Coaching
3. Mentoring
4. Executives—Training of.
5. Leadership—study and teaching. I. Goldvarg, Damian. II. Mathews, Patricia. III. Perel, Norma.

First Edition—First Printing 2018

Author's Note: For simplicity, throughout this book, both coach and client are referred to as "she" though obviously coaches and clients can be of any gender. (Exception: when we quote official International Coach Federation (ICF) materials, we quote them exactly, including constructions like "he or she" and "s/he".) The ICF Coaching Competencies, the ICF Ethical Standards, the Coaching Competency Behavioral Markers, and the Coaching Transcripts have been used with permission. Professional Certified Coach (PCC) is a trademark of the ICF. The names and details of the coaching examples provided in this book have been changed when necessary to respect the confidentiality of the coaching relationships. This book is written for educational purposes only and is not intended for use as any type of psychotherapy, diagnostic instrument, or legal advice.

PRINTED IN THE UNITED STATES OF AMERICA.

Executive College Press
1375 East Grand Ave., #338
Arroyo Grande, CA 93420
(805) 474-4124
www.executivecoachcollege.com

DEDICATION

The book is dedicated to all coaching students and professional coaches committed to keep developing their skills to provide services following high ethical and professional standards.

— Damian and Norma

Norman— Because of his continued support and love through my involvement with ICF, the markers project, the writing of this book, and our journey through life together, he has inspired me more than he will ever know.

— Pat

CONTENTS

PART TWO: CO-CREATING THE RELATIONSHIP

PART THREE: COMMUNICATING EFFECTIVELY

Appendix 3: Coaching Session Transcripts

FOREWORD

C oaching has created a revolution in the nurturing of individuals' personal and professional development. The reader may wonder how coaching caused this monumental shift. After all, speaking with a mature, wise individual to aid one's development is not a novel idea. Our great philosophers, spiritual leaders, psychotherapists, and business consultants provide similar value. This book shows the specific coaching methodology that leads to the transformational development process we call professional coaching.

INTRODUCING THE AUTHORS

I am pleased to help the authors bring this important guide to the public. I met Damian Goldvarg in Puerto Rico at my first International Coach Federation (ICF) global board meeting. Damian went on to become the president of ICF, and I worked alongside him as vice president. He traveled to 38 countries in ten years, tirelessly promoting the value of coaching and teaching the ICF core coaching competencies throughout the world. If there is one individual who has helped the most to promote ICF and professional coaching outside the United States, it is Damian. Accordingly, he received the prestigious ICF Circle of Distinction Award for advancing the profession of coaching in 2018.

Soon after I met Damian, I met Pat Mathews, who was the director of Georgetown University's Coaching Leadership

Program and a fellow ICF global board member. Pat served as vice president of ICF after me and was a key author of the ICF Assessor Resource Guide. Her experience with writing the guide and collaborating with the other members of the ICF Coaching Competency Marker Team shaped her thinking about teaching coaching skills and influenced the writing of this book.

Norma Perel, a well-known Master Certified Coach and mentor coach who co-wrote earlier books with Damian, is well known for her work in demonstrating the ICF coaching competencies. Their guidelines on the coaching competencies, including a related version of this book, were published in Latin America in Spanish and have been widely used in the training of coaches.

I chose to become the executive editor of this book for two reasons—my respect for Damian, Pat, and Norma, and the value I found in their manuscript. This text will fulfill an unmet need by equipping coaches to demonstrate the ICF Competencies at a higher level. I became a more effective coach through studying their reflections and examples of coaching competencies.

DEFINITION OF COACHING

Coaching is the process of partnering with clients in a thought-provoking, inquiry-based process. The client chooses the focus of the conversation and benefits from the coach employing coaching competencies in a confidential relationship, within a formal coaching agreement, to help the client move forward with their most important, self-selected goals.

This inspirational process we call coaching has led the profession to grow rapidly, from approximately 3,000 coaches in

1999 to over 64,000 in 2016, according to the Global Coaching Study conducted by ICF and PricewaterhouseCoopers.

THE DEVELOPMENT OF THE INTERNATIONAL COACH FEDERATION COACHING COMPETENCIES

In 1998, eight coaches, directors, and university professors of coaching programs in the United States met to define the fundamental competencies that a professional coach should demonstrate. The schools that were represented were the Hudson Institute, Newfield Network, Coaches Training Institute, Coach U, Coach for Life, Success Unlimited Network, Academy of Coach Training, and New Ventures West. Their goals were to develop a model that would serve as a guide for the training of new coaches, and to define the parameters required for certification, elevating the credibility of this new profession. The team created a competency model that was independent of the contributors' philosophical approaches and theoretical models, leading to eleven core coaching competencies. These same eleven core competencies are presented in this book, but now complemented by additional helpful detail. These coaching competencies became the basis for much of the curriculum at ICF Accredited Coach Training programs, and the demonstration of these competencies became the basis for passing an oral examination leading to an ICF credential.

However, no peer-reviewed examination of the ICF coaching competencies existed until 2006, when my research was published in the *Proceedings of the Third International Coach Federation Coaching Research Symposium*. This research reported a pilot study showing that coaches supported the ICF coaching competency framework as representing the most important competencies for an effective coach.

Starting in 2011, ICF established a series of committees to re-examine these competencies and identify methodologies to assess them in coaching sessions. The objective of this book is to share the observable behavioral markers of coaching competencies with explanatory commentary and present complete coaching session transcripts to help coaches better utilize the ICF core coaching competencies. Coaches will be better able to assess how well they are using the competencies and learn to refine their use for more successful coaching.

INTRODUCING THE COACHING COMPETENCY BEHAVIORAL MARKERS

The markers are descriptions of specific and measurable behaviors expected to be demonstrated by the coach for each competency at a Professional Certified Coach (PCC) level. The markers were developed to enable assessors to identify the actual behaviors necessary to demonstrate the competency. Previously, assessors relied on statements about each competency that were interpreted differently by assessors in various Accredited Coach Training Program schools and in ICF performance examinations.

How were these markers of competent coaching at the ICF PCC level developed? The markers were created over a three-year period, starting in 2011, by a Markers Core Team consisting of experienced coaches, experienced assessors, and testing and credentialing specialists. The core team was supported by additional ICF volunteers and ICF staff members.

Ultimately, the members of the Markers Core Team were awarded the 2013 ICF President's Award during the team's December 2013 meeting in Prague. Each year, the president of ICF presents an individual or group with the ICF President's Award in recognition of outstanding work to promote coaching in a humanitarian capacity. The Markers Core Team members and 2013 President's Award honorees were Soren Holm, PCC, Hope Langer, MCC, Margaret Krigbaum, MCC, and Patricia A. Mathews, MCC.

At that time, Dr. Damian Goldvarg, MCC, co-author of this book and the 2013 ICF global president, praised the team members, saying, "Over the last two years, the coaches who volunteered for the ICF Markers Core Team have been integral to this project, contributing their subject-matter expertise and hundreds of hours of their time to revise the evaluation system for ICF's credentialing exams and improve training for our body of volunteer assessors. Volunteers are the heart of ICF, and Soren, Hope, Margaret, and Patricia exemplify the dedication and passion that enable us to lead the way in advancing the coaching profession."

Much of the information presented in this volume on the specific behavioral markers of the ICF competencies is an outgrowth of the ICF Assessor Resource Guide for PCC Assessors (May 2016), largely created by Pat Mathews based on the extensive body of work done by the entire core team, including committee members Soren Holm, Hope Langer, and Margaret Krigbaum.

The Association of Coach Training Organizations also conducted numerous conferences and workshops to improve coach educator training to develop new coaches' ability to assess these coaching competencies at a satisfactory level. The association is a nonprofit, global, collaborative organization of coach training organizations—a worldwide community that inspires excellence in coach training and has a mission to cultivate best practices and integrity in coach training.

HOW TO USE THE BOOK

This book consists of four parts, representing the four clusters of ICF Coaching Competencies. Each part is divided into chapters that identify and define each ICF Coaching Competency. Within each chapter, you will find background information on the competency, elements of the competency, the International Coach Federation behavioral markers that must be demonstrated in a coaching session to meet the ICF Professional Certified Coach competency standard, and actual coaching session cases providing examples of those behavioral markers. You will also find a list of additional resources to help you investigate the specific competency further. In the appendices, the authors included actual transcribed coaching sessions that have been illustrated to demonstrate the behavioral markers of the competency, as well as the ICF Code of Ethics and the ICF Professional Certified Coach (PCC) Markers.

You will learn how the behavioral markers are used to evaluate if the coach is demonstrating sufficient coaching competence to pass the ICF oral performance exam at the PCC level. This book details multiple examples of evidence of the behavioral markers for each ICF Coaching Competency. The two complete coaching session transcripts in the appendix are provided to assist the reader to develop a deeper understanding of how the

ICF Coaching Competencies, as demonstrated by the behavioral markers, are utilized throughout a coaching session.

To get the most thorough understanding of coaching competencies I recommend that you read the book from start to finish. You will find the competencies come alive through the explanation and examples the authors provide. Coach training programs also find it helpful to use each chapter as a module to develop a deep appreciation for each competency.

ACKNOWLEDGEMENT OF THE BOOK SUPPORT TEAM

I am pleased to acknowledge that this book would not have come to be published in its current form without the stellar support of Katie Farrell. Katie, in her role at College of Executive Coaching, brought her intellectual competence, editing skill, and dedication in meticulously reviewing multiple editions to create an excellent book. She deserves a gigantic thank you. In addition, a special thank you to Dr. Terry Chen for her helpful, precise wordsmithing of key sections. Also, my appreciation goes to Jessica Bangay for her review of the entire book. Thank you to Patricia Schwartz, Lynn Jones and Bobbie Sue Wolk for their review and helpful feedback on early drafts of the book. Their superb experience evaluating coaching competencies as faculty of College of Executive Coaching enabled them to provide essential feedback to aid the reader's experience. Thanks also to Roy Sablosky for his copyediting expertise and to Andrew Antone and Author Imprints for their graphic design to make this an attractive and easy-to-read volume.

Much gratitude goes to Magda Mook, executive director of ICF, and George Rogers, assistant executive director of ICF, for their friendship and support for this project. Also, thanks to ICF for granting permission to us to reproduce the ICF Coaching Competencies, Coaching Competency Behavioral Markers, and Ethics Code. All of these are significant intellectual property of ICF which took many years to create with the help of countless ICF member volunteers. A sincere shout out of gratitude goes to all those ICF member volunteers who may not be mentioned individually, but their hard work and dedication has enriched ICF and allowed the profession of coaching to thrive.

This book will be beneficial not only to new coaches, but also to experienced coaches who want to further refine their coaching competencies. All who read this book will become better coaches. Moreover, *Professional Coaching Competencies* will be an important asset to those coaches on the path toward obtaining the added credibility that the ICF coaching credential carries in the global marketplace.

Jeffrey E. Auerbach, Ph.D., MCC
President, College of Executive Coaching

INTRODUCTION

The profession of coaching continues to grow globally. The International Coach Federation (ICF) is a nonprofit organization formed in 1995 and is committed to leading the coaching profession at a global level. ICF has members in 143 countries and has credentialed over 23,000 coaches. ICF is committed to the growth of the profession, and has created both ethical and professional standards.

ICF developed a model comprised of eleven core coaching competencies that are presented in this book. The objective of this book is to share this coaching competency model and the behavioral markers developed to assess these competencies. By sharing our experience as coach supervisors, assessors, and mentor coaches, our aim is to help foster the growth of the coaching profession through the development of effective professionals with high ethical and professional standards.

ICF has focused in the past few years on the strengthening of its assessment of the demonstration of coaching competencies with a focus on the Professional Certified Coach (PCC) candidates. This effort led to the development of behavioral markers for each competency- specific behaviors expected to be demonstrated by the coach for each competency at a PCC level. When a coach is trained in a program approved by the ICF or applies for the ICF PCC credential, she must provide evidence of coaching proficiency in all core coaching competencies. The new "markers" are specific indicators that an assessor will listen for to determine whether the core competencies are demonstrated at the PCC level.

These behavioral markers can be a guide to learning the competencies, but are not intended to be used as a checklist in coaching. The authors recognize the paradox of knowing and understanding the markers, while at the same time not paying undue attention to them, so that one is fully present to the client during the coaching session.

The concepts and explanations presented in this book are perspectives on the ICF's competencies and behavioral markers based on professional experience. Each competency interfaces with the others.

"The implementation of these revised markers has two major benefits," said George Rogers, ICF Assistant Executive Director. "First, they will provide for the consistent assessments of applicants for ICF Credentials. In addition, they will empower ICF assessors with the necessary language to provide concrete, specific and useful feedback regarding a candidate's performance."

Rogers noted that the content being assessed remains the same. "We are not changing the ICF Core Competencies in any way. The new assessment markers are simply a more explicit, consistent way of listening during the PCC performance assessment."

Our aim is to define each competency and provide examples so that they are easier to understand and apply. The coaching sessions from which these examples have been excerpted have been reproduced with the consent of the clients who participated in them.

Part One:
Setting the Foundation

CHAPTER 1   Meeting Ethical Guidelines and Professional Standards

> *The International Coach Federation defines this competency as "understanding of coaching ethics and standards and ability to apply them appropriately in all coaching situations."*

E thical and professional standards are the foundation of credibility and protection of the public for any profession. In coaching, standards establish clear expectations between the coach and the client. Standards also foster consistency in coaching quality among professionals involved in the same kind of work. Understanding and implementing these ethical and professional standards is essential in the practice of coaching. Prospective coaches must not only understand them intellectually, but also be able to make decisions and take action based on them.

BACKGROUND ON ETHICAL GUIDELINES AND PROFESSIONAL STANDARDS

The ICF Code of Ethics (see Appendix) has three parts. The first part defines terms such as "coaching," "client," and "conflict of interest." The second part, Standards of Ethical Conduct, has five sections, addressing professional conduct at large, conflicts of interest, professional conduct with clients, confidentiality/

privacy, and continuing development. The third part is a Pledge of Ethics.

In the application of these professional standards, there are two particular challenges that we will explore. The first is confidentiality. The second is the capacity to clearly communicate the differences between coaching, consulting, psychotherapy, and other helping professions, and the knowledge of when to refer a client to a different kind of professional practitioner.

CONFIDENTIALITY

A primary early responsibility of the coach is to explain in writing, but also often verbally, the generally confidential nature of the coaching conversations and relationships. The coach's first responsibility is to clearly explain to her client that everything that will be talked about during the coaching session is generally confidential, with the exception of certain situations covered in the ICF Code of Ethics, and other exceptions to confidentiality that may be arranged. In most situations, the existence of the coaching relationship itself will often be kept confidential. This means that the coach cannot share with another person the name or personally identifiable information of any client without that client's permission.

The concept of confidentiality is especially important in the complex world of coaching services in organizations. If a coach is hired by an organization, whatever is discussed during the session is generally confidential and should be revealed to others in the organization only with the consent of the client or with advance notice of the limits of confidentiality. For example, it is easy to imagine situations where a coach may become aware of some information that ethically or legally would be important for the coach to disclose; say the client is threatening to physically harm someone, or is an airline pilot and drinks alcohol before working. In these cases, it is important to distinguish confidentiality policies related to the coach, the client, and the sponsor. In this context, by the *client* we mean the person being coached. The *sponsor* is the entity that is paying for the coaching process (more details in Appendix). For these reasons, before beginning the coaching process, it is essential that the coach explain to the client what can and cannot (without the client's consent) be shared with the sponsor or other individuals, and with what exceptions.

When it is appropriate, an effective general strategy is to ask the client what she would be comfortable sharing with the sponsor and to have the client be responsible for that communication. In this case, the client has the choice to decide what to share and what not to share. The clarity of the coaching agreement is critical to the establishment of a trusting relationship with the client. The coach may share information based on the decisions about exceptions to confidentiality that may have surfaced in the coaching agreement. In addition, the coach may need to break confidentiality as required by law or for other ethical reasons, but these exceptions to confidentiality should be generally disclosed in advance. For example, if the client or some third party is demonstrating behaviors that may put others at risk, the coach is able to, and may be required to, disclose that information.

The Coaching Agreement and Confidentiality

In Chapter 2, we will discuss this in more detail, but we cannot overemphasize the importance of the relationship between ICF's professional standards and the establishment of the coaching

7

agreement. A professional coaching relationship is established when coaching includes an agreement or contract that outlines the responsibilities of both the coach and the client. It is recommended that the agreement be put in writing and to specify the roles, objectives, duration, session schedule, responsibilities of coach and client, payment conditions, and contingencies (e.g., if the client should cancel sessions or fail to attend without prior notice). The agreement should also make reference to the client's right to terminate the coaching relationship at any time. Some of these elements, like the coaching fee, would usually be included in the coaching agreement with the sponsor, but not in a coaching agreement with an employee—if the organization was paying for the coaching services.

During the coaching agreement process, the coach should pay attention to her intuition and may refer the client to other professionals, or decline to begin coaching, if the coach has concerns about the client's readiness or whether coaching is appropriate for her. Perhaps the client is not ready, not interested, or otherwise unable to commit to the work that will be involved in the coaching process, or there may be other obstacles in the way of achieving the coaching goals. For example, if the client begins the coaching process by complaining about how the last five coaches have not been able to help her, many obstacles to a positive coaching outcome could exist. Perhaps the client is not really interested in coaching; or does not trust the coaching process; or perceives the coaching as having been imposed or coerced. Perhaps a sufficiently safe and confidential environment has not been created; or the client is not willing to look at, or interested in changing, her own behavior.

During the agreement process, the coach should consider:

- how ready, interested, or committed the client is,
- what other coaching experiences the client has had and how the coaching went, and
- what expectations the client has of the coach and the coaching process.

For more on the coaching agreement, see Chapter 2.

Referrals

The coach should be clear about which issues are appropriate for the coaching process and which ones should be referred to other professionals. Topics related to anxiety, depression, substance abuse, and other pathologies are not covered in the type of coaching detailed by the ICF. According to the ICF, coaching is "partnering with clients in a thought–provoking, creative process that inspires them to maximize their personal and professional potential." If the client's goals for coaching do not fall in this category, the client most likely should be referred to another more appropriate professional, such as a therapist or counselor.

APPROPRIATE TOPICS FOR COACHING

Examples of

Appropriate vs. Inappropriate Topics for Coaching

Which of the following topics are appropriate for coaching?

1. The client would like to be more effective in organizing her activities.
2. The client would like to develop clarity about her professional objectives.

---

3. The client would like to improve her relationship with her boss.

4. The client wants to improve her general level of well-being, including healthy eating and better self-care.

5. The client wants to improve her relationship with her co-workers.

6. The client would like to decide whether to separate from her spouse.

7. The client would like to improve her relationship with her mother, with whom she has not communicated in two years.

8. The client would like to avoid suicidal thoughts.

Answer. Only the first five cases are appropriate for professional coaching. The others would be better addressed by a different class of professional practitioner, such as a psychologist, psychiatrist, therapist, nutritionist, or some other professional who is more appropriate for the person's needs. It is important to note here that it is perfectly acceptable, and potentially quite beneficial, for a person to receive a coach's assistance in achieving a given treatment goal that is prescribed by another professional. For example, a client can hire a coach to receive support in developing self-discipline to enable her to better implement a diet regimen created by a nutritionist. When appropriate, and if the client consents in writing, the coach could communicate directly with other relevant professionals that may be working with the client to discuss how to best support agreed-upon treatment goals.

DIFFERENCES BETWEEN COACHING AND CONSULTING

Organizations often hire coaches to help improve the leadership skills of key staff. In these instances, it is important to draw a clear distinction between the roles of coach and capacity-building consultant. The consultant serves as an expert. In many instances, the coach can perform both roles, but she should clearly explain this difference to the client.

Here is what we mean: A consultant is an expert who offers information and often gives expert advice, based on her experience, in an attempt to support a client. Alternatively, a coach explores challenges or obstacles with a client, through a series of thought-provoking conversations, and works collaboratively with the client to design action plans that will better enable the client to achieve her own goals. The coach asks questions that create insights to support the client to get from where she is to where she wants to go. A coach may spend more time helping the client *learn* than a consultant would.

ETHICS CASE STUDY QUESTIONS
What Would You Do?

Case 1. A client calls you to receive coaching and begins to share with you a story of a negative experience she had with another coach who is a colleague of yours. You trust your colleague's ability and intuitively deduce that the client has unrealistic expectations about coaching. Do you take on the person as a new client? What are the alternatives? How would you handle this situation?

Case 2. A client you have been working with for several months says that at work he has been assigned a new coach, but he would like to continue working with you. Is it ethical to continue the coaching relationship knowing that the client will

---

be receiving free coaching at work? What would you ask your client in this situation? What factors do you need to consider?

Case 3. A client who is happy with your work would like to introduce you to her boss so that you might become her boss's coach as well. Would you accept the invitation? Why? If not, why not? What are some of the challenges that could arise out of accepting work with your client's boss?

Case 4. A client who is grateful for your services invites you to her house to meet her family because the transformation she has experienced has also changed her home life. You have worked virtually with your client for six months, and this would be the first time you have met her in person. Would you accept the invitation? Why or why not?

Case 5. A colleague confides in you that another colleague copied his website information for personal self-promotion/marketing. What would you recommend?

Case 6. You notice that a colleague portrays himself as having received an ICF credential when you know that to be untrue. What do you do?

Case 7. A client calls you and says that she feels depressed and wants to cancel today's session. What do you do? Would you charge her for the session anyway?

Case 8. A client owes you payment for the last three months' sessions. Would you offer to provide new sessions or wait until the client pays you?

Case 9. A potential client calls you and says she would like a coach but is not sure about working with you because she would like a coach of the same gender. What do you do?

Case 10. A client offers to write a positive reference about your work on your LinkedIn page. Do you accept? Why or why not?

Now that you have completed these exercises, please note that there are no specific ICF markers for ethical behavior, but there are two behaviors that will disqualify an applicant for a credential (in the review of a coaching session submitted for an ICF credential), even if the markers of the competencies are otherwise demonstrated at the Professional Certified Coach level. The ICF markers are the indicators that an ICF assessor is trained to listen for to determine which ICF Core Competencies are in evidence when an applicant submits a recorded coaching session for the ICF PCC credential. The disqualifiers for the first competency, meeting Ethical Guidelines and Professional Standards, are (1) the coach exhibits a breach of ethics as defined by the ICF Code of Ethics; or (2) the coach more than occasionally steps into a role other than coach (as defined by the ICF), such as consultant, teacher, mentor, or counselor. The ICF takes ethics seriously and requires three hours of ethics continuing education to renew an ICF credential.

FOR FURTHER READING

Jeffrey E. Auerbach, "Inviting a Dialogue about Core Coaching Competencies," *Proceedings of the Third International Coach Federation Coaching Research Symposium*, 2006, 55–70.

Jeffrey E. Auerbach, *Personal and Executive Coaching: The Complete Guide for the Mental Health Professional* (Arroyo Grande, CA: Executive College Press, 2001).

Alexandra Barosa-Pereira, "Building Cultural Competencies in Coaching: Essay for the First   Steps," *Journal of Psychological Issues in Organizational Culture* 5 (2014), 98–112. doi:10.1002/jpoc.21141

Peter Bluckert, *Psychological Dimensions of Executive Coaching* (Maidenhead: Open University Press, 2006).

Lloyd E. Brotman, William P. Liberi, and Karo,l M. Wasylyshyn, "Executive Coaching: The Need for Standards of Competence," *Consulting Psychology Journal: Practice and Research* 50:1 (1998), 40.

Michael Carroll and Elizabeth Shaw, *Ethical Maturity in the Helping Professions* (London: Jessica Kingsley, 2012).

International Coach Federation, *2016 ICF Global Coaching Study*, Executive Summary, Lexington, KY.

Frode Moen and Roger A. Federici, "Perceived Leadership Self-Efficacy and Coach Competence: Assessing a Coaching-Based Leadership Self-Efficacy Scale," *International Journal of Evidence Based Coaching and Mentoring* 10:2 (2012), 1–16.

CHAPTER 2 Creating the Coaching Agreement

> *The ICF defines this competency as the ability "to understand what is required in the specific coaching interaction and to come to agreement with the prospective and new client about the coaching process and relationship."*

C reating a coaching agreement is one of the competencies that sets the foundation of the relationship between the coach and client. It is closely related to the competency of meeting ethical guidelines and professional standards, examined in the first chapter. The ability to effectively establish the coaching agreement between coach and client is essential to the practice of coaching and is also a professional standard. Plus, there are several ethical and professional challenges that can arise during the course of the coaching relationship that have to do with how seriously and clearly the coach and client established that initial coaching agreement.

BACKGROUND ON CREATING THE COACHING AGREEMENT

There are two levels of agreements: the working agreement that outlines the terms and conditions of the coaching process in general, and the agreement that gets established in every session. There should be an alignment between them.

The coach needs to understand and explain clearly to the client the boundaries and concrete parameters of the coaching relationship (logistics, fees, calendar, third-party participation, and so on). Also, the agreement needs to clearly state what is appropriate and inappropriate in the professional relationship, the limits to confidentiality, what is provided as part of the coaching service, and the respective responsibilities of the client and the coach.

ESTABLISHING AN AGREEMENT AT THE BEGINNING OF THE COACHING PROCESS

From the very first contact with the client, the coach listens to the client's needs and interests, and then evaluates what she has heard in making a determination of whether or not to initiate a coaching process. If the coach decides to offer her services, it is recommended that the coach provide the client with a written agreement form to help clarify for both the coach and the client what to expect from the process.

A written agreement clarifies and formalizes the coaching process and increases the client's commitment to it. In addition, discussing key elements of the coaching process (for example, expectations, objectives, coach's and client's responsibilities, and confidentiality) can reduce the chance of misunderstandings later. If differences in understanding around the coaching agreement arise in the coaching relationship, the written agreement can be consulted. For example, if a client does not show up to the coaching session, and does not call in advance to cancel, the coach may or may not have the right to charge for the session, depending on how the agreement was structured. The clearer the agreement, the more these kinds of situations will be prevented.

The coach can locate many sample coaching agreements on the Internet. It is recommended that the coach have the agreement reviewed by legal counsel before asking clients to sign it.

ESTABLISHING AN AGREEMENT AT THE BEGINNING OF EACH SESSION

During every session, the coach needs to work with the client to understand what it is that the client wants to achieve, before thinking of ways to work with the issue presented. Inexperienced coaches often jump right into trying to solve client problems and exploring alternative courses of action without taking the time to explore the client's needs, desires, and expectations of the session.

Exploring the client's concerns allows a coach to determine whether the concerns might be symptoms of another problem. It is important to dedicate sufficient time to developing the coaching agreement to ensure that the coach is working on the issues that will enable the client to accomplish her goals and develop new awareness. This also helps prevent remaining at a superficial level with a client where no real exploration occurs.

Consider the following questions with the client when establishing the coaching agreement and link them to the issues at hand:
- What do you want to achieve in this session?
- Why do you want to achieve this?
- What would you like to work on today?
- What would you accomplish in the next 30 minutes that would make for a successful session?

- How would you know if your objectives were achieved at the end of the session?
- What makes this important to you?
- What is the motivation to work on the concern presented?
- What makes the concern meaningful to you?
- How much urgency do you feel to work on this issue?
- What might you need to resolve to achieve your goal?
- What would you like to be different for you at the end of the session?
- What topics should you explore to accomplish your goals?

These questions are not meant to be a formula for establishing a coaching agreement—they are suggestions and should not sound mechanical. For example, instead of a general question like, "What makes this important to you?" it's usually possible to ask something more specific, like, "What about developing a better relationship with your colleague is important to you?" The coach needs to use the client's own language and expressions to customize the session agreement in partnership with the client. Exploring these questions may help determine the depth of each session.

At the PCC level, the coach focuses on what the client would like to work on, and explores how success might be measured. A professional coach is aware that it is important to explore not only what the client brings to the session, but also what's underneath her motivations. For example, for the client who wants to start going to the gym, the coach may explore not only the benefits this would bring to the client, but also what it means for the client to exercise and what is in the way of her starting this practice. You might ask, for example, "How would your life change as a result of going to the gym?"

Spending a significant amount of time on the coaching agreement can cause a client to worry that time is being taken away from the coaching itself. It is important to iterate to the client that establishing the coaching agreement is part of the coaching process. The coaching session begins from the point where the client starts sharing ideas and concerns about what to work on.

Furthermore, the client might suggest a number of topics on which to focus, one after the other, without much clarity. In this case, it is important for the coach to request that the client choose one topic to work on and reserve the rest of her concerns for exploration in future sessions. It is essential to focus attention on the precise topic as presented by the client, which the client considers a priority. Sometimes the coach needs to ask for specificity. She may ask: "What specifically would you like to work on in relationship to this issue?"

The coach needs to be mindful of the agreement throughout the session and help the client explore ways to progress toward what she wants to accomplish. This should include checking back with the client during the session and at the end of the session to assure that the agreement is still in alignment with the client's stated goal.

We are very sensitive to the use of language by the coach. We believe that the coach should use the client's language and be intentional when asking questions. For example, at the beginning of the session, the coach might ask the client, "What do you want to work on?" This language focuses on taking action, in contrast to, for example, "What topic would you like to discuss today?" By asking about the "topic," the coach keeps the conversation at a merely descriptive level, missing the opportunity to challenge the client to identify concrete actions that can be committed to by session's end. The coach's task is to maximize the client's ability to achieve greater effectiveness by clarifying goals and exploring obstacles, instead of "discussing topics."

Measuring Session Accomplishments
Answering the coach's question of how progress might be measured enables both coach and client to capture the client's ideas of what might constitute an ideal resolution for the session. It is important to differentiate the current state of the client from what might be an achievable goal for the coaching session. The client can clarify ideas, make a decision, begin or stop an activity, or find alternative activities that are not accessible at the moment. Other possibilities include:

- Set a new goal
- Identify the next step of an existing goal
- Identify a hidden obstacle
- Identify and replace negative beliefs or assumptions that are holding the client back
- Create new beliefs that empower the client
- Identify helpful resources
- Create a shift in perspective
- Figure out what to do differently
- Identify what personal strength the client needs to engage more consistently with
- Get clear about what the client really wants
- Get clear about what the client needs to commit to

- Identify "who" the client needs to be to become more effective in this situation
- Find a way to hold the client accountable
- Retire or bust old, unhelpful storylines
- Align the client's language, values, and behaviors
- Set new behaviors for challenging situations

MARKERS OF PROFICIENCY IN CREATING THE COACHING AGREEMENT

According to the ICF, creating the coaching agreement includes the following key behaviors:

1. Coach helps the client identify, or reconfirm, what s/he wants to accomplish in the session.
2. Coach helps the client to define or reconfirm measures of success for what s/he wants to accomplish in the session.
3. Coach explores what is important or meaningful to the client about what s/he wants to accomplish in the session.
4. Coach helps the client define what the client believes he/she needs to address or resolve in order to achieve what s/he wants to accomplish in the session.
5. Coach continues conversation in direction of client's desired outcome unless client indicates otherwise.

The excerpts presented as evidence for each coaching competency marker are *examples* of the type of exchange that can be taken as such evidence. The reader may find more examples. The number of evidence items for each marker will vary depending on the content of the coaching session; the reader should not expect to find equal amounts of evidence for each marker. These observations apply to all the tables in this book. Excerpts of

21

the coaching session are presented in the in-chapter tables and the complete coaching session transcripts can be found in the Appendix.

Case One Examples

COACHING COMPETENCY BEHAVIORAL MARKER	EVIDENCE FROM COACHING CASE ONE
1. Coach helps the client identify, or reconfirm, what s/he wants to accomplish in the session. • Confirms and articulates back the agreement or focus for the session. • Asks the client to define the desired outcome for the session.	2:00 There is an issue you want to be coached on? Describe what you have on your mind. 2:00 I'll play it back and make sure I've got it right. 24:00 Okay, so let's just check in for a minute, because at the beginning you said you wanted to talk about this, you wanted to come to a resolution with some strategies of how to handle it. Where are you now with those strategies? Let's just check in.
2. Coach helps the client to define or reconfirm measures of success for what s/he wants to accomplish in the session. • Asks what the evidence of success would look like. • Reflects back to the client the success measure(s) for the session.	3:00 What would you like to walk away with at the end of our session?

COACHING COMPETENCY BEHAVIORAL MARKER	EVIDENCE FROM COACHING CASE ONE
3. Coach explores what is important or meaningful to the client about what s/he wants to accomplish in the session. • Inquires about the personal and/or professional relevance and/or significance of the client's topic. • Uses questions to help the client clarify what achieving the outcome would mean.	4:00 What is most important to you about this issue?
4. Coach helps the client define what the client believes they need to address or resolve in order to achieve what s/he wants to accomplish in the session. • Inquires about what issues would allow complete achievement of the goal. • Reflects heard issues back to the client. • Explores what must be resolved for the goal to be achieved.	24:00 Okay, so let's just check in for a minute, because at the beginning you said you wanted to talk about this, you wanted to come to a resolution with some strategies of how to handle it. Where are you now with those strategies? Let's just check in. 26:00 Is there anything else you have to resolve in yourself before you go into that conversation? 32:00 As we finish up, then, is there anything else about this that will help you get to the resolution that you want? 39:00 Is there something you wished would've happened that didn't? An area I could've explored but I didn't?

COACHING COMPETENCY BEHAVIORAL MARKER	EVIDENCE FROM COACHING CASE ONE
5. Coach continues conversation in direction of client's desired outcome unless the client indicates otherwise. • Recognizes emergence of new and/or competing session goal and recontracts as needed, and as desired by client, the coaching session agreement and success measures.	*There were no new or competing goals identified and no recontracting was necessary. As seen in the transcript, the coach continued the conversation in the direction of the client's outcome.*

Case Two Examples

COACHING COMPETENCY BEHAVIORAL MARKER	EVIDENCE FROM COACHING CASE TWO
1. Coach helps the client identify, or reconfirm, what s/he wants to accomplish in the session. • Confirms and articulates back the agreement or focus for the session. • Asks the client to define the desired outcome for the session.	1:00 So let's focus on what you want to accomplish today. By the end of the session, what would you like to see differently regarding your leadership? 1:00 How will you know you feel OK with it?

COACHING COMPETENCY BEHAVIORAL MARKER	EVIDENCE FROM COACHING CASE TWO
2. Coach helps the client to define or confirm measures of success for what s/he wants to accomplish in the session. • Asks what the evidence of success would look like. • Reflects back to the client the success measures for the session.	1:30 How will you know that you feel okay with it? 1:30 So by the end of the session today, because this is what you are going to accomplish in the future when you are with your team, but by the end of the session, specifically, what will you want to accomplish around your leadership?
3. Coach explores what is important or meaningful to the client about what s/he wants to accomplish in the session. • Inquires about the personal and/or professional relevance and/or significance of the client's topic. • Uses questions to help the client clarify what achieving the outcome would mean.	3:00 What makes this important to you today? What makes building this confidence and trusting yourself, why is this important for you today?

COACHING COMPETENCY BEHAVIORAL MARKER	EVIDENCE FROM COACHING CASE TWO
4. Coach helps the client define what the client believes they need to address or resolve in order to achieve what s/he wants to accomplish in the session. • Inquires about what issues would allow complete achievement of the goal. • Reflects heard issues back to the client. • Explores what must be resolved for the goal to be achieved.	4:30 Where would you like to start exploring all of the things you are bringing up here? Because you talk about confidence, you talk about trust; you talked about believing in your people. You talked about remembering that you have your own resources. Where do you think will be a good place?
5. Coach continues conversation in direction of client's desired outcome unless the client indicates otherwise. • Recognizes emergence of new and/or competing session goal and recontracts as needed, and as desired by the client, the coaching session agreement and success measures.	*At no time did the client or the coach change direction or need to recontract.*

SPECIFIC CONSIDERATIONS IN CREATING THE COACHING AGREEMENT

Another key coaching behavior to display during the agreement and throughout the session with a client is to clarify the meaning of the words she is using. By understanding the meaning of the words, the coach can develop greater insights into how the client views her circumstances or situation. For example, the coach may ask the client, "What do you mean by the word 'leadership'?" We recommend this kind of exploration of the meaning of words because it can greatly improve the coach's understanding of what it is that the client wants to work on, and because it helps ensure that the client and coach are talking about the same thing.

Finally, at the end of the coaching agreement, the coach or the client may articulate in her own words her understanding of what the client would like to achieve during the session. In Case 1, the coach says:

> It's the issue of... I'll play it back and make sure I've got it right. This is a colleague that you've had for a long time. She's now in your building, and you've done a lot of work for her pro bono, it's getting more and more, and it's taking more of your time. She runs a big business, and yet... You haven't charged her, and you're resentful. You kind of want to charge her, but something's holding you back.

Marker 4 (coach helps the client define what the client believes he/she needs to address or resolve in order to achieve what s/he wants to accomplish in the session) is often not addressed at the very beginning of a coaching session, primarily because the client may not yet know what she needs to address or resolve to achieve what she wants to accomplish in the session. This may be the very focus of the session and will happen later in the session. That said, it is still part of the coaching agreement.

In this chapter, we discussed the coaching agreement as one of the competencies that sets the foundation for the relationship between the coach and the client. In the next chapter, we look at the first of two competencies that establish the coaching relationship: creating trust and intimacy with the client.

FOR FURTHER READING

Tatiana Bachkirova, *Developmental Coaching: Working with the Self* (Maidenhead: Open University Press, 2011).

W. Chalmers Brothers, Jr., *Language and the Pursuit of Happiness: A New Foundation for Designing Your Life, Your Relationships & Your Results* (Naples, FL: New Possibilities Press, 2005).

Sandra Foster and Jeffrey E. Auerbach, *Positive Psychology in Coaching* (Arroyo Grande, CA: Executive College Press, 2015).

Part Two:
Co-Creating the Relationship

CHAPTER 3 Creating Trust and Intimacy

> *ICF defines this competency as the ability "to create a safe, support-ive environment that produces ongoing mutual respect and trust."*

E stablishing trust is essential to the coaching relationship. When there is no trust between the coach and client, it is difficult for the client to open up and to share ideas and concerns. Trust comes from the safe space that is created when the coach demonstrates that she is reliable, can refrain from judging the client, and considers the client whole and complete. When these elements are in place, the client is much more like-ly to feel understood and safe sharing any ideas without fear of being rejected or judged negatively.

BACKGROUND ON TRUST AND INTIMACY

Let us consider the literature that discusses the creation and importance of trust, specifically German philosopher Martin Heidegger, entrepreneur Fernando Flores, leadership expert Steven M. R. Covey, and coach Rafael Echeverría.

In his book *Being and Time*, Heidegger asserts that the only thing that is certain is death. We do not know when or how it will happen, but as soon as we are born, we are already old enough to die. Because we are never far from this fundamental vulnerability in relation to our existence, trust plays an important role in keeping us calm and balanced. When there is trust we have greater confidence, feeling more protected and less vulnerable. When there is no trust, threats often appear exaggerated (see Richard Polt's *Heidegger, an Introduction*). This mentality can lead to a feeling of being in near-constant danger—always vulnerable—and aversion to taking bigger risks. If someone inspires trust in me, it means I have confidence that she has my best interests at heart. It means that I know she will care about the things that are important to me, will take into consideration my worries and concerns, and will not do me harm. She will support me. This feeling of trust is fundamental to the coaching relationship.

The competency of establishing trust and intimacy is defined by the ICF as the ability to create a safe environment. When the client feels confident, safe, supported, accepted, and respected, she has a higher likelihood of committing to the coaching process. The client is willing to "open up" and discuss wide-ranging topics because she feels comfortable and secure, knowing that the coach will support and accept her unconditionally. In *Building Trust in Business, Politics, Relationships and Life*, Robert Solomon and Fernando Flores write, "Trust is something we do, that we create, maintain with our promises, commitments, emotions and sense of integrity. Trust is a choice, a decision."

Trust begins with an assessment. If we carry a positive judgment about the client and the process, and we believe in ourselves, we will help instill trust in our clients. This will support clients in opening up, being vulnerable, and talking about the work they have to do to reach their goals. It is a decision the coach makes, not only about what she has to do, but also about how she is deciding to "show up." When the coach decides to be confident, generous, and kind, and projects a peaceful demeanor, she engenders a trusting relationship with the client. "People aren't about to hand over a part of their future to someone who they don't trust," points out Fernando Flores (in *Conversations for Action and Collected Essays*).

In *The 7 Habits of Highly Effective People*, Steven Covey writes, "Trust is the highest level of human motivation. It attracts the best in people but it takes time and patience." The author often uses an "emotional bank account" metaphor, in which he explains that what adds to the trust account is acts of courtesy, honesty, and generosity, and the maintenance of commitments. Covey identifies a variety of other ways to increase trust deposits, such as demonstrating devotion, clarifying expectations, exhibiting integrity, and genuinely apologizing when one makes a mistake. All of the above practices should be applied by the coach.

FOUR KEY ELEMENTS OF TRUST

In *The Speed of Trust*, Steven M. R. Covey identifies four key elements in the development of trust that can be applied during the coaching process.

The first element is integrity. It is related to the amount of consistency we maintain between what we say and what we do, and the way we are perceived by others. As coaches, we are required to respect the joint commitment between client and coach. If we are not on time, or if we fail to follow through on something, we are making withdrawals from the trust account. This is especially important during the outset of the coaching process, given that our first sessions will define and set the tone of the coaching relationship. Failing to build trust and integrity in these formative first meetings could result in the client deciding not to continue the coaching relationship.

The second element presented by Covey is intention. How effective are we at clarifying our intentions? Are we clear in defining expectations with our clients? This is essential to the coaching agreement, because the clearer the coach can be in defining and conveying exactly what is expected in the coaching relationship, the safer the client will feel. This is of paramount importance in laying a foundation for productive collaboration between coach and client.

The third element is capacity, which includes knowledge, abilities, talents, and personal style. When the coach has the training, credentials, and appropriate level of experience, the likelihood that she will be perceived as credible is at its highest. For example, the ICF requires accredited coaches to take 40 hours of continuing education, including three hours in ethics and professional standards, to renew their credential. This requirement demonstrates to current and future clients that the coach is committed to expanding her coaching knowledge and to personal and professional growth.

The fourth element is results. When the coach works with clients whose productivity improves, this fosters credibility. In particular, client testimonials to the coach's effectiveness can greatly enhance a coach's marketability. Continued training, and the appropriate abilities and skills, will aid in the development of trust.

TWO SIDES OF TRUST

In his book *La Empresa Emergente* (The Emerging Company), Rafael Echeverría writes that trust has two sides: assessments and emotions.

When I say Juan is trustworthy, that is an assessment—a belief or opinion I have about Juan. It may be a factual statement, meaning I have some evidence for it. Or it could be extra-factual, for example if others have influenced me to think of Juan as trustworthy. This type of judgment will influence the type of relationship I end up developing with Juan, just as it will affect the way I speak about Juan when I'm talking about him to others. The problem comes when we take assessments as fact, and proceed as though what we believe or think we know about Juan (without actual evidence) is, without a doubt, the truth.

If one side is judgment (assessment), the other side of trust is emotional. When I say Juan is trustworthy, I'm conveying that I feel calm in his presence. In essence, when I'm around Juan, my emotional state changes. If I think Juan is not trustworthy, I will feel uncomfortable around him, and I will behave differently. I might be less likely to be open with Juan, and more likely to be defensive, nervous, or worried.

TRUST DOMAINS

From the perspective of the coach, the development of trust in the coaching relationship has three key aspects: trust in the client, trust in oneself as coach, and trust in the coaching process.

Trust in oneself means that the coach is secure in the knowledge that she has the requisite training and specific experience to be effective in the role of coach. Experience fosters confidence.

In mentor-coaching groups, coaches that have many years of coaching experience often still seek practice with colleagues to feel more confident at applying the competencies presented in this book.

When a coach is confident, the judgments of others—positive or negative—have little bearing on her opinion of herself, and she does not feel the need to demonstrate how knowledgeable she is about a topic. When these kinds of worries are absent, the coach is more "available" to the client.

Trust in the client means that the coach "demonstrates respect for the ideas, learning style and overall presentation and habits of the client" (Whitworth et al., *Co-active Coaching*). The coach is capable of expressing confidence in the thought process of the client.

The authors of *Co-active Coaching* suggest that clients are "complete" and have all of the answers (or if not the answers, the ability to find the answers). The coach's job is not to "fix" anything about the client, but instead to ask questions and invite self-discovery. Clients are deemed to be creative, capable of finding the resources, and able to generate the questions they need. The coach's job is to be curious without providing consultation. In other words, the role of the coach is not to be an expert, but to remain focused on the client's goals.

Trust in the process means that the coach has confidence that the coaching process works and that, whatever the exact direction of the session, the client will benefit from the conversations that take place. Personally or with her clients, the coach has experienced the power of the coaching transformation, and she knows that coaching can make a difference in clients' lives.

To build trust, the coach can strategically, and confidentially, share stories of what other clients have achieved in the coaching process, or share a personal experience that might allow a client to identify with the coach. Other strategies are to ask questions that demonstrate interest in the client, and to ask clarifying questions that may be questions that the client also has. When the coach asks questions that might be uncomfortable for a client, it is best to first ask the client for permission, to ensure that the client feels safe exploring topics that are challenging.

When there is trust between the client and the coach, intimacy develops—a bond is created. When intimacy develops, clients feel safe enough to share ideas and to be vulnerable. You know this kind of intimacy is present when a client shares her vulnerabilities with you as if she has known you for a very long time.

Building trust and intimacy is about respecting, supporting, and encouraging the client. As you can see in the transcripts, the coaches make specific and supportive comments to create a safe environment. We did not provide specific evidence for Marker 3 (encourage the client to fully express herself) in this chapter because it is demonstrated throughout both coaching sessions (see Appendix).

THE "GOOD COACH" IMAGE

The Professional Certified Coach, while she may have the ability to establish trust and a connection between herself and the client, may be overly concerned with presenting the image of a "good coach." As a result, she may be less willing to take risks.

Trust and intimacy are not truly present when a coach is more interested in her own perspective of what is best for the client than in helping the client to uncover her own. This is often evidenced by little or no effort being made to grasp the client's own perspective of the situation. Neither are trust or intimacy present when the coach's attention is focused on demonstrating knowledge about a topic rather than on inviting the client to share her own ideas, or when the coach sets the direction of a session without asking for the client's opinion. Finally, this competency will not have been demonstrated if the coach displays what appears to be an intention to *teach* during the session instead of coaching the client.

In coaching situations, we may fail to recognize the absence of trust. This can take the form of our belief that the client has truly opened up, when she is really sharing only a part of the story. We may be convinced that a client lacks motivation in her work, when what is really lacking is trust in the coaching process and relationship.

MARKERS OF PROFICIENCY IN CREATING TRUST AND INTIMACY IN A COACHING SESSION

The behavioral markers for this competency are:

1. Coach acknowledges and respects the client's work in the coaching process.
2. Coach expresses support for the client.
3. Coach encourages and allows the client to fully express him/herself.

Case One Examples

COACHING COMPETENCY BEHAVIORAL MARKER	EVIDENCE FROM COACHING CASE ONE
1. Coach acknowledges and respects the client's work in the coaching process. • Relates to the client through eye contact (for in-person or on-camera coaching); adapts to or matches client's vocal rhythms; tracks with the client's language (body language or verbal language). • Understands, recognizes, and respects the client's self-concept/identity (the who). • Recognizes and affirms the client's courage and/or willingness to change.	8:00 I love that you have that there, and that's one of the ways you calibrate what you do.
2. Coach expresses support for the client. (*Support* is not the same as *caretaking*.) • Makes empathic comments. • Expresses confidence in the client's capabilities. • Reflects the client's progress. • Acknowledges successes, strengths, and unique characteristics.	7:00 Nice. 8:00 I love that you have that there, and that's one of the ways you calibrate what you do. 24:00 That's what makes you a good coach. 31:00 Yeah. That's a big step for you. 36:00 I know it'll be hard, but I'll be rooting here for you.

COACHING COMPETENCY BEHAVIORAL MARKER	EVIDENCE FROM COACHING CASE ONE
3. Coach encourages and allows the client to fully express him/herself. • Uses silence that allows the client to process thinking and feeling. • Invites the client to disagree with the coach. • Affirmatively encourages the client to continue to express herself.	2:00 I'll play it back and make sure I got it right. 2:00 Is that it?

Case Two Examples

COACHING COMPETENCY BEHAVIORAL MARKER	EVIDENCE FROM COACHING CASE TWO
1. Coach acknowledges and respects the client's work in the coaching process. • Relates to the client through eye contact (for in-person or on-camera coaching); adapts to or matches the client's vocal rhythms; tracks with the client's language (body language or verbal language). • Understands, recognizes, and respects the client's self-concept/identity (the who). • Recognizes and affirms the client's courage and/or willingness to change.	*The coach continuously asked the client's opinion and matched client's pace, rhythm, and energy.*

COACHING COMPETENCY BEHAVIORAL MARKER	EVIDENCE FROM COACHING CASE TWO
2. **Coach expresses support for the client.** (*Support* is not the same as *caretaking*.) • Makes empathic comments. • Expresses confidence in the client's capabilities. • Reflects the client's progress. • Acknowledges successes, strengths, and unique characteristics.	10:00 You sound like more confident, you said "be there," like in the way that it came out, it came out like with a confidence you were talking about. 28:00 Congratulations on your work.
3. **Coach encourages and allows the client to fully express him/ herself.** • Uses silence that allows the client to process thinking and feeling. • Invites the client to disagree with the coach. • Affirmatively encourages the client to continue to express herself.	6:30 What is your hypothesis of what is going on there?

THE COMPLICATION OF "MANDATORY COACHING"

One of the most difficult contexts in which to form a trusting coaching relationship is when the coaching is mandatory. The client may not even be interested in participating, or may not understand what coaching is. When organizations send employees for coaching without a clear explanation of why they are being sent, or as a way to "punish" or "remedy" some work-related issue, it is not uncommon for a client to be defensive and not trust the coaching process. It is through clear coaching explanations—about the coach's role, the possible benefits of coaching, the coach's credentials and experience—that the client can appreciate the value of coaching and commit to working on the identified areas.

If it is determined that trust cannot be created due to variables beyond the coach's control, it is important for the coach to decide whether or not to continue working with the person. If the coach suspects the client is not ready to fully participate in the coaching process, she needs to have a conversation with the client or the client's sponsor (respecting confidentiality and recognizing that delivering such a message could harm the sponsor's view of the employee) to convey that assessment, and to attempt to identify alternatives to coaching.

It is important to know the level of the client's commitment to the coaching. She may be committed to her professional growth in general, but not necessarily committed to growth in a particular context just because a manager or family member has recommended that she embark on a coaching process. For these reasons, in situations where the coach has been hired by the organization and not chosen by the client, the development of trust takes on greater importance, which could be overlooked. In this scenario, how might the coach create trust with the client?

One strategy would be to demonstrate genuine interest in the person, not just as an employee of the company but also as a human being, with worries and needs of her own that go beyond the particular work challenge or question the coach was called in to help address. The first conversation relating to coaching that takes place is very important in this regard.

The coach should explain clearly to the client what is expected in the coaching relationship, the coaching methodology, the importance of confidentiality, and any other topic that will clarify for the client what the coaching process entails.

In the next chapter, we discuss the second competency related to developing the coaching relationship: coaching presence.

FOR FURTHER READING

Stephen Covey, *The 7 Habits of Highly Effective People: Powerful Lessons in Personal Change* (Simon and Shuster, 1989).

Stephen M. R. Covey, *The Speed of Trust* (New York: Free Press, 2006).

Rafael Echeverría, *La empresa emergente* (Buenos Aires: Granica, 2000).

Fernando Flores, *Conversations for Action and Collected Essays: Instilling a Culture of Commitment in Working Relationships* (Createspace, 2012).

Martin Heidegger, *Being and Time* (Harper Collins, 1927).

Richard Polt, *Heidegger: An Introduction* (Ithaca, NY: Cornell University Press, 1999).

Robert C. Solomon and Fernando Flores, *Building Trust in Business, Politics, Relationships and Life* (Oxford: Oxford University Press, 2001).

Laura Whitworth, Karen Kimsey-House, Henry Kimsey-House, and Phillip Sandahl, *Co-Active Coaching: New Skills for Coaching People toward Success in Work and Life* (Boston: Davies Black, 2009).

CHAPTER 4

Coaching Presence

> *The ICF defines this competency as the ability "to be fully conscious and create a spontaneous relationship with the client, employing a style that is open, flexible and confident."*

C oaching presence is one of the most important competencies a coach can possess. Being present requires more than a *moment* of close connection; it means a sustained connection, a kind of "bubble" in which client and coach can sit together for a while. Coaching presence focuses on the client as a whole, not only the situation presented, but also how the client relates to the issue, and on the partnership between client and coach.

Coaching presence is closely related to the competency of establishing trust and intimacy. When there is presence, the client feels complete trust toward the coach, and this helps the client open up and share her feelings.

BACKGROUND ON COACHING PRESENCE

We conducted a survey of coaches using LinkedIn, in which we asked, "How do you think a coach should demonstrate coaching presence in a session?" The answers included:

- The coach demonstrates presence by active listening and validating what the client brings to the session, challenging her comfort zone. It is important to challenge the comfort zone and listen carefully.
- Listening at a 200% level. Making the client feel that there is no one else more important than her and her situation. It is fundamental to be available for our clients.
- It is the empathy the coach demonstrates to the client that allows the client to see the commitment of the learning process.
- Being present can be achieved through listening and questioning and by demonstrating that we are here and now at all moments. The coach's presence will determine the relationship that can be created.
- Being present is being here and now with my internal voice, emotions, and body focused on the client, leaving behind thoughts that can interrupt and can take away our presence.
- Being in the here and now allows connecting with the client and being more attentive.
- Being present is being connected with my client with all of my senses: Body, soul, mind, and heart. With everything that makes me be. Finding where the client comes from. Being able to feel what the client feels, being conscious of what we are going through, to be neutral and be cautious of not introducing my agenda to the client's process.

UNPACKING THE DEFINITION OF COACHING PRESENCE

The most fundamental element in the ICF definition of this competency is the coach's ability "to be fully conscious." It means a focus on the here and now, and limiting the internal dialogue and thoughts about the past and future. Being fully conscious also means paying attention to the client's verbal and nonverbal expressions, to one's own personal reactions to the client, and to the context of the conversation.

The second element in the definition emphasizes the relationship. A "spontaneous relationship" refers to the ability to accompany the client to unknown places during the coaching session and co-create the relationship.

"Employing an open, flexible and confident style" refers to the coach's ability to adapt easily to varying scenarios presented by the client, and to depart from her preconceived methods and hypotheses. It implies confidence in herself as well as in the coaching process and its ability to bring about an outcome that is best for the client.

Being "open" means having the ability to explore new territory or unknown territories and be comfortable without knowledge or a clear answer. This is a defining difference between a consultant and a coach. A consultant is a *content* expert who provides advice and guidance based on her experience and knowledge of a particular subject area. The coach is a *process* expert, and may not know about the particular themes the client brings to the sessions. The coach does not need to be a content expert and have answers for all of the issues the client brings. Rather, the coach explores them with the client, and together they may identify undiscovered possibilities.

BREATHING EXERCISE

Breathing Exercise for Coaching Presence

We recommend starting with an exercise that will help you be present throughout the reading of this chapter on coaching presence. After reading this paragraph, we invite you to close your eyes, and inhale and exhale slowly, paying attention only to your breathing. Repeat three deep inhalations and exhalations, slowly. Then open your eyes and focus on how you feel.

The objective of this exercise is to bring you into a state of being present, and it is used by many coaches at the outset of coaching sessions to separate and successfully disconnect from a prior activity. Being conscious of your body and breathing can bring you to the present and increase your ability to focus. This focusing exercise can also be given to a client at the beginning of a coaching session. Invite the client to inhale deeply, focusing on her breathing, and to ignore other thoughts or problems. This allows the client to be totally present.

CREATING COACHING PRESENCE IN THE COACHING PROCESS

Coaching Presence and the Coach's Internal Experience

In his book *Presence-Based Coaching,* Doug Silsbee writes, "The ability to be present is an internal experience that can be developed." He says that there are three doors to being present: the body, the mind (what we think, what we focus on), and the heart. Being present enables us to be more effective, creative, authentic, flexible, and able to deal with challenges. This potential is available to us in every moment of every day; we only need to understand how to access it. To be present means to be conscious of our surroundings, ready to face any situation that might arise, and to have the internal resources to meet the challenge. It also means to listen deeply and to be ready to go beyond our own preconceived ideas in attempting to make sense of our reality. Silsbee defines being present as a state of consciousness characterized by complete surrender (when we are present we do not check the time). There is a connection with our client, the environment, and ourselves. Being present awakens us and allows us to live with less stress. When we are present our internal dialogue diminishes, which is tied to a higher level of consciousness.

Coaching Presence and Mindfulness

There is a story in *The Power of Now* where author Eckhart Tolle makes reference to the importance of mindfulness. He explains the power that comes with the ability to ignore the thoughts that prevent us from being present in the multiplicity of situations we find ourselves in in our daily lives. He tells a story about a monastery where a Zen master tested his disciples by walking behind them and attempting to startle them individually. Those who were "present" were alert to and perceptive of what was going on in their immediate environment, so they were not as startled by the master's sudden presence. Those who were caught up in a cloud of concerns and distracted by their thoughts were startled.

In *Full Catastrophe Living*, Jon Kabat-Zinn defines mindfulness as "moment to moment non-judgmental awareness," which applies to the work of the coach and how she needs to purposefully pay attention to the client, to herself, and to the context.

49

COACHING PRESENCE AND INTUITION

Accessing our intuition is important for coaching effectiveness. What does it mean to access our intuition in the coaching relationship? It means that the coach can interpret information beyond that which the client expresses verbally, and can relate it to what may have been said. It also means that the coach can make sense of non-verbals, such as body language and signals, in the absence of clear verbal information. Intuition is knowing something without necessarily knowing exactly how we know it. Often it is not what the client says, but what she did not say, that leads us to an insight about her. Silence can provide information. Intuition can also involve connecting something that occurs in this session to something we saw in an earlier session with this client. These intuition-based insights can help us formulate the kinds of questions that open up new possibilities or productive pathways (Whitworth et al., *Co-active Coaching*).

An experienced coach is not afraid to follow her intuition, nor is she afraid to take risks and make mistakes. She does not fear asking questions that can make a client feel uncomfortable, so long as she perceives a readiness on the part of the client to head in a direction established in the coaching agreement. The coach's role is to respectfully invite the client to explore terrain the client has never visited, so to speak, but always with the client's permission. The coach is ready and willing to take risks to explore the unknown. The process of coaching does not have to be "clean and perfect."

The coach is not demonstrating presence if all her questions and comments are focused on her own performance. The coach may be too concerned about what will be the next question, as opposed to focusing on the relationship with the client. To be "available," the coach needs to focus not only on results and solutions, but also on the learning process that is occurring throughout the course of every coaching session.

Many coaches have a great deal of concern about what their clients will do after the coaching conversation ends. It is important to implement actions designed during the sessions—but to focus on action for action's sake is to remain at a superficial level of coaching. The professional coach should focus on the client and challenge who that client was when she faced a certain challenge and how she related to this issue. The coach may also explore what is required to acquire a new perspective on the situation by identifying limiting beliefs, fears, or anything that can be in the way of the client accomplishing her goals. In other words, she is able to coach the client and her issue.

The coach is the person who helps the client discover new possibilities for action, not to limit herself to one action. The coach works with the client to explore different activities and open new opportunities for learning. The coach has a variety of tools, and can decide which one may be most suitable for the client in that specific moment. For example, she can recommend breathing exercises, or use visualizations or metaphors, to explore the concerns presented in the session in line with the coaching agreement.

The coach needs to develop the ability to be comfortable around the client's emotions. The coach should be open to embracing and acknowledging the client's feelings and invite her to express and explore them. It is important to give the client space to express strong feelings when necessary. The silence of the coach can be of great benefit on these occasions.

New coaches may think that expression of emotions and managing emotions is a mental health professional's job. We believe that exploring emotions is an important part of the coach's work. To clarify the difference, we would like to differentiate expression of emotions from clinical issues. If the emotions are so strong that they imply significant depression, anxiety, or trauma, the coach should consider a referral, because the client might need the assistance of a licensed mental health professional and the emotions may be beyond the scope of the coaching relationship. This is related to the ethical standard of referring the client to another professional if another type of professional service is warranted. It is important for the coach to recognize emotions, to be able to work with them, and to be present to what the client is feeling in the moment, without fearing the expression of emotion.

MARKERS OF PROFICIENCY IN COACHING PRESENCE

The professional coach follows the client's agenda, and responds to the information relating to actions that might achieve the client's goals. The coach demonstrates partnership with the client. This emphasis on partnership is an important part of professional coaching and is emphasized in the behavioral markers of coaching presence.

If the coach does not inquire about the client's perspective and centers her attention on her own knowledge of the issue, or if she places too much focus on one coaching method or standard questions, the coaching presence competency is not demonstrated at a PCC level.

The ICF states that a coach is demonstrating coaching presence when there is observable evidence of the following behavioral markers:

1. Coach acts in response to both the whole person of the client and what the client wants to accomplish in the session.
2. Coach is observant, empathetic, and responsive.
3. Coach notices and explores energy shifts in the client.
4. Coach exhibits curiosity with the intent to learn more.
5. Coach partners with the client by supporting the client to choose what happens in the session.
6. Coach partners with the client by inviting the client to respond in any way to the coach's contributions and accepts the client's response.
7. Coach partners with the client by playing back the client's expressed possibilities for the client to choose from.
8. Coach partners with the client by encouraging the client to formulate his or her own learning.

Case One Examples

COACHING COMPETENCY BEHAVIORAL MARKER	EVIDENCE FROM COACHING CASE ONE
1. **Coach acts in response to both the whole person of the client and what the client wants to accomplish in the session.** • "Whole person" includes, for example, when or how the client thinks, creates, and relates.	4:00 That's how you're feeling now? [*Indicates interest not only in the issue but also in the person.*] 5:00 Yeah. Does this sound like anything else that goes on in your life, or is it just this one situation? [*Coach is interested in the person beyond this specific challenge.*] 12:00 Yeah. Okay, so you thought about… You've taken some practical steps toward a log, knowing how many hours, thinking about asking to get paid for that, yet something's still holding you back. What do you think that is?

COACHING COMPETENCY BEHAVIORAL MARKER	EVIDENCE FROM COACHING CASE ONE
2. **Coach is observant, empathetic and responsive.** • The coach treats the client's emotions respectfully, responsibly, and with unconditional positive regard.	8:00 I love that you have that there, and that's one of the ways you calibrate what you do. 10:00 Wow. Yeah, so it really feels unequal now. 11:00 Yeah, so you want to be valued. You want to be valued for the work you do, and value has something to do with finance at this point, which... For sure. 12:00 Let me understand. If you were to make an offer of a retainer of a certain amount per month, she'd give you more... It's sort of like, again, being undervalued, right? She'd give you more work than that retainer would normally cover.

COACHING COMPETENCY BEHAVIORAL MARKER	EVIDENCE FROM COACHING CASE ONE
3. **Coach notices and explores energy shifts in the client.** • Shares observational feedback with the client when the client's vocal, verbal or body rhythms change.	17:00 Yeah. If I could just kind of break this apart a minute, I saw your face when you said, "I coach her a lot too," and there seemed to be something about that that didn't... I don't know. It wasn't the same as when you said you loved the coaching and you coach her staff. There's something in there. 23:00 Okay. What I heard from you clearly, and your facial expressions, is that the first two you have no problem putting a value on, ... The third one... I don't know, I heard a little ambivalence there in terms of, "How would I ever value it?"
4. **Coach exhibits curiosity with the intent to learn more.** • Genuinely and authentically inquires about the client's agenda. • Genuinely and authentically inquires about aspects of the client as a person.	10:00 What's at risk for you if you draw a boundary in this situation? 12:00 What's at risk for you if she's annoyed?

COACHING COMPETENCY BEHAVIORAL MARKER	EVIDENCE FROM COACHING CASE ONE
5. Coach partners with the client by supporting the client to choose what happens in the session. • Extends an invitation to co-design or co-create session focus and direction. • Checks in on focus and direction during the session.	3:00 What would be helpful? 4:00 That's how you're feeling now? 11:00 OK, what do you want? 24:00 Let's check in for a minute.
6. Coach partners with the client by inviting the client to respond in any way to the coach's contributions and accepts the client's response. • Partners with the client by, if offering assessments or opinions, doing so as an invitation for the client to use or not use, as the client sees fit. • Hears and respects the client's frame of reference and thinking and, as appropriate, shares her own thinking and frame of reference without attachment.	5:00 You're acknowledging it's a lot your fault, yet you're waiting for her to make an offer? 11:00 So you want to be valued? 20:00 Yeah. I'm kind of hearing, if I can play back this to you. I'm kind of hearing three buckets, and I don't know, tell me if that's what you mean, because maybe those offers are different for different buckets. One bucket is HR work, right? That bucket, it sounds like you don't have any ambivalence at all about counting up the number of hours and asking for a reasonable amount of pay. Would that be right?

COACHING COMPETENCY BEHAVIORAL MARKER	EVIDENCE FROM COACHING CASE ONE
7. Coach partners with the client by playing back the client's expressed possibilities for the client to choose from. • Recognizes and reflects when, where, and with whom the client is at choice. • Paraphrases or clarifies coach's understanding of choices by the client.	19:00 Yeah. I'm kind of hearing, if I can play back this to you. I'm kind of hearing three buckets, …. One bucket is HR work, right?… Would that be right? 23:00 Okay. What I heard from you clearly, and your facial expressions, is that the first two you have no problem putting a value on, …. The third one… I don't know, I heard a little ambivalence there in terms of, "How would I ever value it?"
8. Coach partners with the client by encouraging the client to formulate his or her own learning. • Inquires about and/or champions the client's capability to assess her learning. • Inquires about the client's intuition and interpretation of client's being, situation, and/ or actions.	32:00 Is there anything else about this that will help you get to the resolution you want? 37:00 What learnings did you have from the session?

Case Two Examples

COACHING COMPETENCY BEHAVIORAL MARKER	EVIDENCE FROM COACHING CASE TWO
1. Coach acts in response to both the whole person of the client and what the client wants to accomplish in the session. • "Whole person" includes, for example, when or how the client thinks, creates, and relates.	3:00 It is in the context within the last sessions of who you want to be as a leader.
2. Coach is observant, empathetic and responsive. • The coach treats the client's emotions respectfully, responsibly, and with unconditional positive regard.	10:00 You sound like more confident, you said "be there," like in the way that it came out, it came out like with a confidence you were talking about.
3. Coach notices and explores energy shifts in the client. • Shares observational feedback with the client when her vocal, verbal or body rhythms change.	10:00 Isn't the thing because in your voice different than before. You sound like more confident; you said "be there," like in the way that it came out, it came out like with a confidence you were talking about.
4. Coach exhibits curiosity with the intent to learn more. • Genuinely and authentically inquires about the client's agenda. • Genuinely and authentically inquires about aspects of the client as a person.	16:00 That voice was telling you to wait, where do you think it was coming from?

COACHING COMPETENCY BEHAVIORAL MARKER	EVIDENCE FROM COACHING CASE TWO
5. Coach partners with the client by supporting the client to choose what happens in the session. • Extends an invitation to co-design or co-create session focus and direction. • Checks in on focus and direction during the session.	4:30 Where would you like to start exploring all of the things you are bringing up here? Because you talk about confidence, you talk about trust; you talked about believing in your people. You talked about remembering that you have your own resources. Where do you think will be a good place? 5:00 Okay, so inside of you, around what question would you like to answer or explore?
6. Coach partners with the client by inviting the client to respond in any way to the coach's contributions and accepts the client's response. • Partners with the client by, if offering assessments or opinions, doing so as an invitation for the client to use or not use, as the client sees fit. • Hears and respects the client's frame of reference and thinking and, as appropriate, shares her own thinking and frame of reference without attachment.	21:00 What you're saying is it's about trusting people, is that it? 26:00 Just to make a comment, so when you're asking questions you said a couple of things that I wanted to bring to your attention. 27:30 I am asking you also if you want to consider as a possibility how you can use this not only for your work as a volunteer but also in your personal life.

COACHING COMPETENCY BEHAVIORAL MARKER	EVIDENCE FROM COACHING CASE TWO
7. Coach partners with the client by playing back the client's expressed possibilities for the client to choose from. • Recognizes and reflects when, where, and with whom the client is at choice. • Paraphrases or clarifies coach's understanding of choices by the client.	4:30 Because you talk about confidence, you talk about trust; you talked about believing in your people. You talked about remembering that you have your own resources.
8. Coach partners with the client by encouraging the client to formulate his or her own learning. • Inquires about and/or champions the client's capability to assess her learning. • Inquires about the client's intuition and interpretation of client's being, situation, and/or actions.	16:30 Okay so how do you think that this what you're saying affects your leadership? What happened when this was coming from your heart different than from your head? How does this affect who you are as a leader?

FURTHER NOTES ON PRESENCE

In these last two cases, we can observe how the coaches showed curiosity and empathy and effectively developed a partnership with the client. The coaches inquired not only about the situation, but also about what was happening for the client in relation to the situation.

Each of the 11 key competencies of the ICF can be associated with an image or a word. We like to associate presence with a couple dancing the tango. When there is presence, what we observe is a couple dancing harmoniously. When they are struggling, it looks like dancers going in opposite directions.

Presence Exercises
Every person is different, and what works for one might not work for another. Breathing exercises can be helpful. Breathing exercises are simple to explain, easy to perform, and effective. When we are worried or stressed out, bringing ourselves into a present state of mind allows us to set those thoughts aside, and to focus only on our inner experience, our respiration, our body, and, in turn, to become "centered." It has been proven that focusing on our breathing for as little as one minute a day is effective for increasing focus (Whitworth et al., *Co-active Coaching*).

Meditation is another great tool. Practicing it every day for 10 minutes in the morning and 10 minutes in the evening gives us opportunities to be more present in our lives. It is a useful tool in countering stress and tension. The challenge comes in finding and committing the time to meditate.

The chapter on mindfulness in Wildflower and Brennan's *Handbook of Knowledge-Based Coaching* offers a list of practices for use in coaching. These include maintaining an authentic and nonjudgmental presence, maintaining your focus on the client during the session, helping the client practice mindfulness, meditative reading, yoga, tai chi, connecting with nature, and listening to music.

Internal Distractions
Sometimes we have the client in front of us, but instead of listening to her, we are more focused on the voice inside us. These

thoughts could be reflections on what we think might be going on with the client, solutions that might benefit the client, or simply our own emotional reaction to what she is telling us. Our thoughts might even be focused on situations unrelated to the coaching session (such as personal problems or a different client's problems).

The Need to be Liked

The need to be liked can distract us from the work at hand. Worrying about whether we're liked or accepted reduces our ability to be present and authentic. We have seen coaches who are so concerned about being liked by their colleagues and their clients that they lose their presence. They are afraid of being ineffective or embarrassed, and so they miss opportunities to be fully present. The thought that the client might stop liking her can stop a coach from challenging the client in the way the client actually needs.

Confidence and Performance

Confidence and presence go hand in hand. When the coach is not confident in her abilities, confident in the client, and confident in the process, she loses presence because she is more concerned about being effective than simply doing her job.

Being more focused on performance than on what the client brings to the session can be an obstacle to coaching presence. The challenge is how to remove these thoughts from our minds. This is important not just when we are coaching, but also in our lives in general. Our fears, anxieties, and worries limit our presence. These prevent us from enjoying life or being present in the moment. Once we can identify these unproductive thoughts, we need to set them aside and focus our attention and energy on our client's experience. In order to stop this kind of internal dialogue, we have to identify the unproductive thoughts, and then change them into something more productive.

Organizational Issues

There are external factors that can interfere with the coach–client relationship and take away from the coach's presence. For example, having had a client referred to her by a colleague, a coach might wonder how that colleague perceives her skill level, which diverts some of her attention and mental energy during the coaching session. This reduces the coach's presence for the client. Another example is we might be overly concerned about what the client's manager thinks of our skill level or approach. It is also possible for information we have regarding the client and her organizational context to be an obstacle to being completely present with her. If we are able to identify these obstacles, we can stop them and quiet this internal dialogue. It is up to us as coaches to choose to focus our thoughts and our attention on what is occurring with the client. Paying attention to our body and our breathing helps us to be present.

"Virtual" Conversations

"Virtual" conversations are a special challenge. Since coach and client are not in the same physical space, the coach needs to pay attention to other behaviors such as breathing, tone of voice, silence, energy shifts, and external noises. When working by telephone or other virtual modalities, the coach needs to develop skills beyond only words to show understanding to the client. If a coach is not practiced at delivering coaching virtually, practice and reflection on her coaching performance usually brings enhanced skill. Coaching supervision can be a good place to reflect on our work in situations in which we lack experience.

In the next chapter, we explore the competency of active listening, one of the group of competencies under "communicating effectively."

FOR FURTHER READING

Janet Baldwin Anderson, Francine Campone, and Jennifer Sellers, "Mindfulness," Chapter 21 in *The Handbook of Knowledge-Based Coaching: From Theory to Practice*, edited by Leni Wildflower and Diane Brennan (San Francisco, CA: Jossey-Bass, 2011).

Jon Kabat-Zinn, *Full Catastrophe Living: How to Cope with Stress, Pain and Illness Using Mindfulness Meditation* (Bantam, 1990).

Amanda Ridings, *Pause for Breath: Bringing the Practices of Mindfulness and Dialogue to Leadership Conversations* (London: Live It, 2011).

Doug Silsbee, *Presence-Based Coaching: Cultivating Self-Generative Leaders through Mind, Body, and Heart* (Wiley & Sons, 2008).

Eckhart Tolle, *The Power of Now: A Guide to Spiritual Enlightenment* (Sydney: Hachette, 2009).

Laura Whitworth, Karen Kimsey-House, Henry Kimsey-House, and Phillip Sandahl, *Co-Active Coaching: New Skills for Coaching People toward Success in Work and Life* (Boston: Davies Black, 2009).

Leni Wildflower and Diane Brennan, *The Handbook of Knowledge-Based Coaching: From Theory to Practice* (Jossey-Bass, 2011).

Part Three:
Communicating Effectively

Active Listening

CHAPTER 5

> *The ICF defines this competency as the ability "to focus completely on what the client is saying and is not saying, to understand the meaning of what is said in the context of the client's desires, and to support client self-expression."*

he ICF emphasizes that to communicate effectively the coach needs three competencies: active listening, powerful questioning, and direct communication. In this chapter, we focus on active listening, which is closely connected to the previous chapter's topic, coaching presence. As we have explained in earlier chapters, all competencies are interconnected. Being present means quieting the internal voice to be fully focused on what the client is communicating. As a consequence, the coach's listening is focused on the client and not on the coach's own inner voice.

BACKGROUND ON ACTIVE LISTENING

The ICF presents the following behaviors as key elements of active listening:

- "By actively listening, the coach focuses on the client's agenda without imposing her own agenda." She focuses one hundred percent on the client's issues, priorities, and themes. The client takes the lead in the conversation. The coach might feel tempted to bring to the conversation her personal opinions and judgments about what the client should focus on, but it is preferable not to do so. It is important for the coach to be conscious of what she says and does and to be careful not to impose her own perspectives.

- "The coach listens to client's concerns, goals, values, and beliefs about what is possible." The coach pays attention to the limiting beliefs and thoughts that the client has about herself and her situation. If it is appropriate, she can challenge those beliefs, always with the client's permission. For example, the coach can ask: "Would you give me permission to challenge something you just said?"

When the coach "listens" and hears that the client is not taking action on a stated goal, the coach might explore the costs of the beliefs that limit the client from taking action. In certain situations, it might also be valuable to explore the hidden benefits of those beliefs (see Chalmers Brothers, *Language and the Pursuit of Happiness*).

For example, a client states the goal of the session is to change her negative perspective of men to a positive one. Her ex-boyfriend emotionally abused her, and that has led to her negative view on starting a new relationship. When someone introduces her to someone new, she thinks negatively about that person. When she is asked, "What benefits do you get from thinking that way?" she replies that by thinking negatively, she is protecting herself from getting hurt again. This could mean that her internal conversations have blocked her from the possibility of developing a new relationship with a man. That hidden benefit impedes her from having a positive outlook toward men. By being aware of her beliefs and challenging them, she can be more effective in dealing with her challenges.

- "By actively listening, a coach can distinguish between words, tone of voice, and body language." For example, the client might say that something is not bothering her but say it with an angry tone of voice. It might be appropriate for the coach to observe, "You said you were not angry, but your tone of voice sounds angry. What do you think?" Sometimes body language can say a lot. If we observe something that seems inconsistent with the content of the comment, we may challenge our clients.

  Some potential questions or comments might be: "You look rigid, not as relaxed as usual. Do you think your body is telling you something? If so, what?" "Do you feel rigid, or is it only my observation?" or "Your voice changed when you talked about your friend. What emotions do you get when you talk about her?" These questions are examples that can help the client explore the body language and foster consciousness of the differences in her body and verbal language. Many times, clients do not have a sense of their body language, and pointing it out allows them to effectively register it.

- "To ensure clarity and understanding, the coach summarizes, paraphrases, reiterates, and reflects what the client says." All of these strategies help the coach show understanding of what the client is saying. If we said what we said, and the others heard what they heard, the only way to know that we understood what was said is to check. This is not a given. When we ask for clarification or share our understanding of what we just heard, we limit miscommunication. Summarizing and synthesizing are techniques that help the client and the coach clarify and identify what was discussed. Paraphrasing, stating back what was heard in the coach's own words, also helps the client reflect. When the coach acts like the client's mirror, it can help the client open interpretative spaces that were not present previously. For example, in the dialogue presented below, when the coach functions as a mirror, she helps the client notice what is behind what she is bringing up.

In our coach training, we hear amateur coaches repeat what the client just said, not for the benefit of the client, but because they don't not know what else to say. It is also not appropriate to paraphrase multiple times in a coaching conversation. It is expected that the coach uses a variety of tools to demonstrate active listening.

- "The coach encourages, accepts, explores, and reinforces the client's expression of feelings, perceptions, concerns, beliefs, and suggestions." The coach supports the client's self-expression. Being vulnerable and opening up can be challenging. Throughout our lives, we may have experienced negative consequences for speaking our minds. By listening actively and showing unconditional regard, the coach helps the client express herself honestly, genuinely, and without fear of being judged. The following dialogue is a good example:

> **Coach:** Tell me, how you are feeling now?
> **Client:** The first thing that comes up is that I feel I'm someone who is good person, passionate for what I do, and focused on helping other people, but I am afraid that will be misinterpreted. [Client starts crying]

Coach: I appreciate you being vulnerable and willing to explore your beliefs and emotions. What is on your mind?

Client: I am concerned about being judged negatively.

Coach: I can hear your concerns. Tell me more.

Client: Yes, I realized my fears are not founded.

Coach: Tell me more about it.

Client: These fears come from past experiences, and are not related to my current challenge.

In this dialogue, the coach invites the client to express herself without limitations. The coach is not frightened by the expressions of the client's emotions, but invites the client to explore her beliefs and emotions.

- "The coach integrates and builds on the client's ideas and suggestions." The coach summarizes her understanding of the client's concerns and helps the client focus her agenda. In general, we do not want to interrupt the client. However, sometimes it becomes necessary, particularly when the client talks about unnecessary details, perhaps to avoid difficult or challenging topics. In these circumstances, we may have to interrupt the client and ask for a summary.

- "The coach allows the client to come to a resolution without judgments or attachments, in order to move on to next steps." The coach can have her own ideas about the client's issues, but she should work on having the client find her own solutions independently, without the coach's opinions or judgments. The coach can be tempted to share some ideas, especially if she is an expert on the theme or knows of resources that can be useful to the client. In those cases, after the client explores her beliefs and alternative actions, the coach can offer some suggestions with the client's consent.

We would like to distinguish between giving advice and sharing knowledge. If a coach is asked for information, for example, and has some knowledge about an appropriate and perhaps helpful resource, she should feel free to offer the resource, partnering with the client to determine whether it would be helpful. If the coach is an "expert" in an area that the client seeks advice on, she needs to avoid taking over the session in a consultative fashion and offering advice to the client. This advice may be based on the coach's experience, but it is not a partnered coaching move. For example, if you are working with a client who is struggling with strategic planning, and you have been doing that work for years as a consultant, you may be tempted to take over and guide the process. Instead, the coach may offer a suggestion and partner with the client so the process becomes one of the client's design and not the coach's.

HEARING AND LISTENING

The coach not only hears, but also listens. Hearing and listening are two different activities. Hearing is a physiological capacity. I can hear without listening, not paying attention to what was said. Listening is about understanding and showing that understanding. The coach needs to pay attention not just to what is spoken, but also to the unspoken, the context, and possible meanings. In *Language Acts*, Rafael Echeverría explains that to listen is to perceive with all of the senses and to interpret, giving meaning to what is heard. To do this, we need to understand not only the expressed words, but also the context.

All interpretations are made from a personal historical perspective, and are based on judgments, assumptions, and pre-conceived notions. Every interpretation is relative. It does not describe the facts, but provides a subjective meaning that is not absolute. It is composed of judgments that are neither true nor false. The problem arises when we take our interpretations as the truth. The coach needs to pay attention to her interpretations and to be cautious regarding when to share them with the client. The coach can offer interpretations as a hypothesis, but it is useful for the client to arrive at her own hypothesis and meaning.

Echeverría asserts that listening is parallel to talking and is what guides the communication process. Therefore, listening is not a passive action, as is usually believed. Talking and listening are two different phenomena that can lead to gaps in under-standing. Each one of us interprets what we hear. That may lead to misunderstandings, so verifying what we just heard is import-ant in the coaching process. He offers three resources to narrow the gap:

Verify our listening. Paraphrase what the client says, with similar words, to make sure that the coach's listening is aligned with what the client expressed to avoid interpretations. Synthesize what the client says.

Explore underlying concerns. It is about listening for something underneath what the client is saying, something that was not expressed. The coach may intervene to help the client focus on her underlying concerns.

Inquire to refine, correct, and complete what we hear. Listening is the key to effectively working with your client. Listening is about valuing the other person and being curious and interested in the meaning behind her words.... If we don't feel heard, we don't feel valued.

It is important for the coach to be conscientious of the filters she uses in listening to the client. When we talk about filters, we refer to preconceived ideas that we have about reality that influence and determine how we understand what the client is telling us. Being conscious and recognizing that the meaning we give to words and concepts is a result of our history allows us to realize the possibility that the meaning the coach and the client give to concepts may be different. Therefore, the best way to understand the meaning that the client intends is by asking a question such as: "When you say that it is difficult for you to do it, what makes you think it is difficult? What does difficult mean to you?"

Every concept can have different meanings and interpretations, according to our culture, past experiences, and beliefs. Knowing this can help us clarify what we are speaking about and what our client is telling us. For example, if the client says, "Today, I want to work on being more organized at work," an effective coach might ask, "What does being organized mean to you?" or "What do you mean when you say 'organized'?" There is an exercise we do in communication trainings, where we say a word and ask participants to visualize it. If we say "cat," everyone visualizes a different cat, as a result of their different experiences and education.

When we are conscious of our filters or biases, we work more effectively as coaches. Positive Psychology focuses on people's strengths and not their weaknesses. When a listening filter is "positive," the coach pays special attention to what is working well rather than what is not working (for more on this, see Foster and Auerbach's *Positive Psychology in Coaching*).

In a virtual class for the ICF in 2010, Elena Espinal explained how listening generates the context for something to occur in the session. The way we listen will affect what can or cannot happen during the session. We can hear the mental games our clients employ when they talk about their development; their values and meanings; what is possible and what is not; what decisions they can make; what they want to convince us of; and what they do not want us to ask them. A client may say she wants something, but when we start exploring that, we may suspect that this is a false belief: she doesn't really want it. Do you think that, as a coach, you listen to the person as someone who can succeed even though you don't know her? Are you able to double-listen, listening to the client and to yourself from where you are, being aware of your own filters and emotions?

Our listening ability depends on our filters as we work with our clients. What we can't distinguish, we won't be able to recognize or explore. Our ability to distinguish depends on our listening, our coach training, on the theoretical underpinning, and on our professional experiences.

In previous chapters, we discussed how active listening is necessary throughout the coaching session. Presence, trust, and intimacy allow us to create an appropriate space for partnership, active listening, and powerful questioning that helps create awareness in the client.

MARKERS OF PROFICIENCY IN ACTIVE LISTENING

The ICF states that a coach is demonstrating active listening when there is observable evidence of the following behavioral markers:

1. Coach's questions and observations are customized by using what the coach has learned about whom the client is and the client's situation.
2. Coach inquires about or explores the client's use of language.
3. Coach inquires about or explores the client's emotions.
4. Coach inquires about or explores the client's tone of voice, pace of speech or inflection as appropriate.
5. Coach inquires about or explores the client's behaviors.
6. Coach inquires about or explores how the client perceives his/her world.
7. Coach is quiet and gives client time to think.

Case One Examples

COACHING COMPETENCY BEHAVIORAL MARKER	EVIDENCE FROM COACHING CASE ONE
1. Coach's questions and observations are customized by using what the coach has learned about who the client is and the client's situation. • Listens to client processes, not only the specific meaning of client's language and concepts. • Uses what the client has said to form questions, not only about the situation but about the client's being.	2:00 Okay. It's the issue of... I'll play it back and make sure I've got it right. This is a colleague that you've had for a long time. She's now in your building, and you've done a lot of work for her pro bono, it's getting more and more, and it's taking more of your time. She runs a big business, and yet... You haven't charged her, and you're resentful. You kind of want to charge her, but something's holding you back.

COACHING COMPETENCY BEHAVIORAL MARKER	EVIDENCE FROM COACHING CASE ONE
• (continued)	4:00 Tell me at what point in this relationship it went from "I'll do her a favor," to being taken for granted.
	10:00 Wow. Yeah, so it really feels unequal now.
	11:00 Yeah, so you want to be valued. You want to be valued for the work you do, and value has something to do with finance at this point, which… For sure.
	12:00 Yeah. Okay, so you thought about… You've taken some practical steps toward a log, knowing how many hours, thinking about asking to get paid for that, yet something's still holding you back. What do you think that is?
	22:00 Okay. What I heard from you clearly, and your facial expressions, is that the first two you have no problem putting a value on, asking for it is another thing. We'll get to that in a second. You have no problem putting a value on that. The third one… I don't know, I heard a little ambivalence there in terms of, "How would I ever value it?" Well, if she was anyone else how would you value it?

COACHING COMPETENCY BEHAVIORAL MARKER	EVIDENCE FROM COACHING CASE ONE
2. Coach inquires about or explores the client's use of language. • Uses or incorporates the client's actual words into coach's paraphrasing, summarizing or questioning.	5:00 You're acknowledging it's a lot your fault, yet you're waiting for her to make an offer? 6:00 When you say you talk about it, you mean when you get angry enough you confront the situation then, and you draw some conclusions? 11:00 What's at risk is she might be annoyed, she might underpay you, right? She might offer something …
3. Coach inquires about or explores the client's emotions. • Asks about or reflects the client's emotions by recognizing mood, tone, affect, images or values.	4:00 That's how you're feeling now? 6:00 When you get angry about it, what happens? 7:00 When you say you talk about it, you mean when you get angry enough you confront the situation then, and you draw some boundaries? 33:00 Right, I can see that all over your face.

COACHING COMPETENCY BEHAVIORAL MARKER	EVIDENCE FROM COACHING CASE ONE
4. Coach inquires about or explores the client's tone of voice, pace of speech or inflection as appropriate. • Shares observational feedback when the client's vocal intonation or verbal pacing changes.	22:00 Okay. What I heard from you clearly, and your facial expressions, is that the first two you have no problem putting a value on, asking for it is another thing. We'll get to that in a second. You have no problem putting a value on that. The third one… I don't know, I heard a little ambivalence there in terms of, "How would I ever value it?" Well, if she was anyone else how would you value it? 37:00 When you say it now, you seem more confident than you did before.
5. Coach inquires about or explores the client's behaviors • Shares observational feedback when the client's vocal intonation or verbal pacing changes.	35:00 Good. That's kind of what I was thinking about is that… Back to your concern that she might offer you something too little, because clearly you got too little for that.
6. Coach inquires about or explores how the client perceives his/her world. • Asks about, identifies, or tests the client's beliefs, assumptions, values, and perspectives.	5:00 Does this sound like anything else that goes on in your life or is it just this one situation? 35:00 Good. That's kind of what I was thinking about is that… Back to your concern that she might offer you something too little, because clearly you got too little for that.

COACHING COMPETENCY BEHAVIORAL MARKER	EVIDENCE FROM COACHING CASE ONE
7. When appropriate, coach is quiet and gives client time to think. • When listening to a response, coach gives sufficient time for the client to answer.	6:00 *Prior to this question, the coach was quiet.* 7:00 *Prior to "nice," coach was quiet.* *There are many other examples where the coach gave the client time to answer. These are not always identifiable from the transcript.*

Case Two Examples

COACHING COMPETENCY BEHAVIORAL MARKER	EVIDENCE FROM COACHING CASE TWO
1. Coach's questions and observations are customized by using what the coach has learned about whom the client is and the client's situation. • Listens to client processes, not only the specific meaning of client's language and concepts. • Uses what the client has said to form questions, not only about the situation but also about the client's being.	18:00 I heard in this conversation a couple of times where you had some realizations. One when you talk about discovering who you really are as a leader before people have figured out who you are like you knowing yourself.

COACHING COMPETENCY BEHAVIORAL MARKER	EVIDENCE FROM COACHING CASE TWO
2. Coach inquires about or explores the client's use of language. • Uses or incorporates the client's actual words into coach's paraphrasing, summarizing or questioning.	5:00 Okay, so inside of you, around what question would you like to answer or explore? 9:00 The lighthouse, I think. Or [foreign language] in Spanish, yeah. 9:30 So if you will be a lighthouse and you guide like in the middle for the boat how would that look like and how would you show up as a leader? 27:00 How is it in a nice way, in a very nice way how is it?
3. Coach inquires about or explores the client's emotions. • Asks about or reflects the client's emotions by recognizing mood, tone, affect, images or values.	*Missed opportunity*
4. Coach inquires about or explores the client's tone of voice, pace of speech or inflection as appropriate. • Shares observational feedback when the client's vocal intonation or verbal pacing changes.	10:00 Isn't the thing because in your voice different than before. You sound like more confident; you said "be there," like in the way that it came out, it came out like with a confidence you were talking about.
5. Coach inquires about or explores the client's behaviors • Asks about the client's actions; reactions; or responses to people, places, or events.	16:30 How does this affect who you are as a leader?

COACHING COMPETENCY BEHAVIORAL MARKER	EVIDENCE FROM COACHING CASE TWO
6. **Coach inquires about or explores how the client perceives his/her world.** • Asks about, identifies, or tests the client's beliefs, assumptions, values, and perspectives.	1:30 It seems that one of the talents is to remember that, is it? 3:00 Trusting you is also related to what you said before about being more confident as a leader. 6:30 What is your hypothesis of what is going on there? What do you think is coming, that "need" that people will think like you, do with you? 16:00 And that voice, sorry for interrupting you, but that voice was telling you to wait, where do you think it was coming from? 16:30 Okay so how do you think that this what you're saying affects your leadership? What happened when this was coming from your heart different than from your head? How does this affect who you are as a leader? 21:30 What you're saying is it's about trusting people, is that it? That you're trusting people even without seeing them.
7. **When appropriate, coach is quiet and gives client time to think.** • When listening to a response, coach gives sufficient time for the client to answer.	*During the entire session, the coach gave the client time to answer. This is hard to determine just from the transcript. A few examples are at 3:30, 5:00, 8:30, and 17:00.*

In this chapter, we presented the key elements of active listening. In the next chapter, we explore a competency that is closely related: powerful questioning.

FOR FURTHER READING

W. Chalmers Brothers, Jr., *Language and the Pursuit of Happiness: A New Foundation for Designing Your Life, Your Relationships & Your Results* (Naples, FL: New Possibilities Press, 2005).

Rafael Echeverría, *Actos del Lenguaje, Volumen 1: La Escucha* (Buenos Aires: Granica, 2008).

Elena Espinal, Virtual presentation, International Coach Federation, 2010.

Fernando Flores, *Conversations for Action and Collected Essays: Instilling a Culture of Commitment in Working Relationships* (Createspace, 2012).

Sandra Foster and Jeffrey Auerbach, *Positive Psychology in Coaching* (Arroyo Grande, CA: Executive College Press, 2015).

CHAPTER 6 — Powerful Questioning

Powerful Questioning

> The ICF defines this competency as the ability "to ask questions that reveal the information needed for maximum benefit to the coaching relationship and the client."

Powerful questioning is important to the process of helping clients reach their potential. For many coaching students, formulating powerful questions is one of the most difficult skills to develop because it requires a high level of sophistication and the application of other key competencies, such as active listening, presence, and direct communication. Powerful questioning does not mean memorizing a list of questions. Rather, it means customizing questions to the unique situation presented by the client.

BACKGROUND ON POWERFUL QUESTIONING

Here are the key elements of the competency:

1. "The coach asks questions that reflect active listening and the client's point of view." Active listening enables the coach to ask exploratory questions that will help create new possibilities. Powerful questioning and active listening are intimately connected. We cannot ask powerful questions if we have not been listening actively and if we are not present

during the coaching session. Therefore, there are no standard "powerful questions." This competency focuses on asking questions that arise from what the client presents during the coaching session.

2. "The coach asks questions that generate new insights, new perspectives, new commitment, and new possibilities for action." This competency is closely related to the competency of creating awareness, because greater awareness comes as discoveries are made by the client in her attempts to answer the coach's questions. Powerful questioning challenges assumptions and beliefs, and encourages reflection.

3. "The coach asks open-ended questions that allow for increased clarity and create new possibilities or new lessons." Greater clarity can be beneficial not only when it is about the specific situation brought by the client, but when it also applies to other areas of the client's life. The deeper the learning, the more opportunities the person will have to apply what was learned to other areas of her life. If the coach asks too many closed-ended questions or yes/no questions, she may limit the client's thinking and answers.

4. "The coach formulates questions that enable the client to advance to her objective, instead of looking back, or making justifications about the past." It is important to focus the questions on the future—to experience the client's past only as a means of exploring experiences that can be useful for the future, not as a way of identifying explanations. For example, "What makes this issue important to you today?" might be a more helpful question than "Why is this issue important to you?" "Why" questions can also make a client defensive.

CHARACTERISTICS OF POWERFUL QUESTIONING

How do we know when we are questioning powerfully? Based on our experiences, powerful questioning:

- Creates an impact, moves the client to action, and can be transformative.
- Illuminates and takes the client to places she has never been before, creating new possibilities.
- Produces an insight, a realization of something she may never have noticed before.
- Creates awareness. The client makes connections she had not made before.
- Temporarily removes the client from the story to take her to the future.
- Enables the client to reflect.
- Can cause the client to say, "That is such a good question!" or "What an interesting question!"
- Can produce exclamations such as "Aaaaah!" (indicating both surprise and recognition) or responses like "I would have never thought of that," "No one has ever asked me that," or "Since you asked me that, I've noticed that…"

What are the key components of powerful questioning?

- Curiosity is very important to effectively investigate and explore what is really going on with the client. In this way, the coach does not assume the role of an expert. This is the difference between a professional coach and a consultant, whose role it is to provide advice or suggestions (Whitworth et al., *Co-active Coaching*).
- As coaches, we are not experts. We are committed to exploring and learning together, with the goal of aiding the client's

discovery of what is possible for her. The coach and the client become colleagues, and, indeed, partners. By being at the same level in this way, we, as coaches, are co-creating and generating new possibilities for action alongside the client.

- Coaches may not influence clients with their own beliefs. In a situation where the coach might want to offer an opinion, suggestion, interpretation, or share her ideas, she can do it through a question. She can inquire as to whether the idea might work for the client, without attachment to her idea. The temptation to provide personal opinions is always present, so the coach needs to be conscious of her own biases and preferences.

- If it becomes very difficult for the client to answer a question, the coach can rephrase it. An experienced coach allows time for the client to reflect when a powerful question is asked. The coach is comfortable with silence and gives the client space to take time to think and process information and question at her own pace.

- Curiosity and the ability to be open to exploration are what enable powerful questioning. In our experience as coaches and mentors, we have seen that less experienced coaches are often afraid to ask questions that might make their clients feel uncomfortable. It is important for coaches to keep in mind that if trust is in place, the client knows that the coach is committed to working at developing her potential. With this trust comes an increased opportunity to open up a space for true exploration. This is one of the biggest challenges because it calls for focusing not only on the *what*, but also on the *who*.

THE DIFFERENCE BETWEEN THE *WHAT* AND THE *WHO*

The *what* refers to what the client would like to work on. For example, the client might say, "What I want is to be more effective at managing my time. I am not very organized, and I want you to help me to learn how to manage my calendar and activities." This is what the client wants. However, if we ask powerfully, we will explore not only what the client wants to do or find out, but also *who* the client is, what is happening that might be preventing her from being or getting organized, how the client perceives the problem she has with getting organized, and what emotional reactions she might have about the issue. The result of this exploration may be a very powerful and transformative experience. If the coach stays only on the *what*—in this case, how to be more organized in managing a calendar—the coaching work will remain at a superficial level.

Through exploring *who* the client is and *what* is on her mind, the coach can begin to identify ways of fostering different results. It is possible, for example, that underlying the apparent inability to get organized are challenges that relate to issues of self-esteem. For example, a client who has difficulty saying no, and instead agrees to almost every request, may find it difficult to complete projects and manage her time. Another possibility is that the client is afraid of failure, or even of success. Indeed, there could be an array of factors that come together to define *who* the client is being, and if the coach explores these, the insights gained might be much more profound and valuable than if she focuses just on the *what* (in this case, organizing activities).

The coaching agreement may change during the session as a result of this deep co-exploration. In this case, it is important to communicate effectively to reach a new agreement between coach and client.

In order to question powerfully, the questions should be clear, concise, to the point, and asked one at a time. If questions are stacked—asked one right after another—the client may feel as though she has to choose one, and this will usually be the last one that was asked. If the questions are shorter, clearer, and more precise, they will tend to be answered more effectively.

HOW TO QUESTION POWERFULLY

The coach asks questions that focus on the future, not the past; she is comfortable taking risks, and she's not afraid to ask the kinds of questions that might make the client uncomfortable. The coach also allows the client to formulate her own questions. If the answer to a question is known by the coach, it is important for the coach to be careful not to steer the client in any direction. Instead, the coach needs to be able to co-explore new possibilities. It is important to evaluate underlying messages and thought processes, and to learn from the client. Our creativity helps us ask more powerful questions. We need to work on developing our creativity and outside-of-the-box thinking to be better able to challenge our clients (Whitworth et al., *Co-active Coaching*).

Other aspects to take into consideration when asking powerful questions are:
- the sequence in which questions are asked;
- the tone of voice used when asking;
- the location and placement of emphasis when asking; and

- the use of language. In formulating questions, it is important to show or ask with care, to be able to choose the words that will have the greatest impact on the client.

In *Coaching Questions*, Tony Stoltzfuls points to some types of questions we should avoid:

- Questions that are, or could be judged to be, "formulaic" or "standard." Sometimes coaches think they should have a prepared set of questions that can be asked during the session. It is better to be totally present with our clients and to explore what each one brings to the session, relying more on our listening skills to formulate questions. There are a few standard-sounding questions that can be used, but they should be used sparingly, and sensitively. Two such questions are, "How are you feeling?" and "What do you think your responsibility is in this situation?"
- Closed-ended questions (ones which can be answered yes or no). These risk taking clients to predetermined places, thereby closing off opportunities for exploration or preventing clients from opening up. Examples of closed-ended question include, "Can you, in reality, take charge of that?" and "Do you have another option?" To avoid formulating closed-ended questions, try starting with the word "how" or "what". The following examples are open-ended questions: "How would your life change if you were in charge of that?" and "What other options would you have?" If you realize that you have just asked a closed-ended question, following it with an open-ended one is a good technique to utilize.
- Questions which include solutions or advice. In general these are closed-ended. They often begin with phrases like

"shouldn't you," "could you," "can you," or "did you." Take the question, "Have you talked to your boss about it?" It allows only yes or no for an answer—and implies that one of these is preferable. Perhaps the coach in this case knows which answer *she* would prefer. An unbiased, open-ended way to ask might be: "In your company, what are the channels of communication for resolving problems?" Another example of this kind of inherently limiting question is, "Can you find a friend you can go to the gym with?" Alternatively, a coach might ask, "What would help to make you more disciplined in going to the gym?"

- Rhetorical questions that can imply judgment or the coach's opinion. "Are you really going to let that opportunity pass you by?" "Wouldn't you like to have a better relationship with your client?" "What were you thinking when you made that decision?" There are more effective ways of asking such things. "What else do you think may be happening?" "What would be the advantages and disadvantages of making that decision?" In situations like these, it is important to recognize and understand what we, as coaches, are thinking and feeling, and to keep our tendency to form judgments about the client in check.

- Questions that have interpretations embedded in them. For example, "How long ago did you start disliking your job?" If a coach does not know with certainty that the client dislikes her job, then the wording reveals a judgment about the client. We can only be 100% certain of something having to do with a client if it is something she told us. The best approach is to use the client's own words. If a client says "I feel frustrated," we should not interpret, but rather ask,

"How long have you felt frustrated?" Or a better question might be, "What makes you feel frustrated?"

- Questions that begin with "why" often elicit defensive reactions, or an impulse to justify past actions or behaviors. They can also lead to a generalized resistance in the coaching session. Questions like, "Why did you do that?" and "Why did you leave your work?" would better be modified to "What factors led you to leave your job?" Also, asking why can send a client back to the past, and risks giving the impression that you believe that there is, in every instance, a clear, linear, cause-and-effect explanation for why things turn out the way they do in life.

JUDGING QUESTIONS AND LEARNING QUESTIONS

In *Change Your Questions, Change Your Life*, Marilee Adams suggests that our thoughts, in general, occur in response to all the questions we continually ask ourselves. If we pay attention to the way we think, we notice that our thoughts come from internal questions, which can create new possibilities and perspectives in our lives.

Adams distinguishes between two types of questions, which she calls *learning questions* and *judging questions*. "What is wrong?" "Whose fault is it?" "How can I test whether I am right?" "Why does this happen to me?" These are all examples of what one could call reactive, or judging questions. While it is quite normal to want to ask them, if we can replace them with learning questions, we can find greater well-being in our lives. The learner asks, "What can I do in this situation?" "What can I do to get what I want?" "What am I responsible for?" "What do I want to learn?"

According to Adams, if we can recognize the judging questions, acknowledge them, and then let go of them, we can formulate learning questions and create new possibilities for progress. This distinction is powerful for our coaching work. When a client asks judging questions and not learning ones, it is a good opportunity to challenge her to analyze what the question is asking and invite her to identify a learning question that might be more helpful in accomplishing her goals.

Powerful questioning brings us to a different place. It is important to be focused on the way we ask a question, and to be precise with the vocabulary we choose. A question about "when you achieve this" is quite different than "if you achieve this." In the latter, the coach implies (unwittingly, perhaps) some doubt as to the possibility of the achievement. A very useful activity we recommend to coaches is to record a coaching session (after first obtaining the client's permission), write down all the questions that were asked, and evaluate which ones were powerful and which ones were not.

In general, the professional coach's questions follow the client's goals and are geared toward obtaining information. They do not stay at a superficial level. They may find a solution to the presented problem, but often they respond more to the client's agenda than to deeper or underlying issues (by referring to "what to do" instead of "who the client is" in a given context or situation). The coach's questions should address both the presented issue as well as serve to probe the deeper issue of who the client is (the situation and the self).

MARKERS OF PROFICIENCY IN POWERFUL QUESTIONING

The ICF states that a coach is demonstrating powerful questioning when there is observable evidence of the following behavioral markers:

1. Coach asks questions about the client; his/her way of thinking, assumptions, beliefs, needs, wants, etc.
2. Coach's questions help the client explore beyond his/her current thinking to new or expanded ways of thinking about himself/herself.
3. Coach's questions help the client explore beyond his/her current thinking to new or expanded ways of thinking about his/her situation.
4. Coach's questions help the client explore beyond current thinking towards the outcome s/he desires.
5. Coach asks clear, direct, primarily open-ended questions, one at a time, at a pace that allows for thinking and reflection by the client.
6. Coach's questions use the client's language and elements of the client's learning style and frame of reference.
7. Coach's questions are not leading, i.e. do not contain a conclusion or direction.

Case One Examples

COACHING COMPETENCY BEHAVIORAL MARKER	EVIDENCE FROM COACHING CASE ONE
1. Coach asks questions about the client; his/her way of thinking, assumptions, beliefs, values, needs, wants, etc. • Inquires about thinking, assumptions, beliefs, and values without necessarily using those exact words in the coaching.	4:00 Tell me at what point in this relationship it went from, "I'll do her a favor," to being taken for granted. 19:00 Is there a loss in there at all for you if you present her with some kind of proposal? 21:00 Well, I don't know. I guess the question is, would you want to if you found a way, or is that something you feel like it's satisfying enough for you to see the growth of her business, and you have a piece in that, or will that continue to make you resentful? 25:00 Okay. How'd that feel when you said it out loud?
2. Coach's questions help the client explore beyond his/her current thinking to new or expanded ways of thinking about himself/herself. • Questions and observations challenge the client's thinking. (Not in all sessions.) • Questions and observations move client out of the current story she is telling and help her look forward.	5:00 Yeah. You're acknowledging it's a lot your fault, yet you're waiting for her to make an offer? 6:00 When you get angry about it, what happens? 7:00 When you say you talk about it, you mean when you get angry enough you confront the situation then, and you draw some boundaries? 10:00 What's at risk for you if you draw a boundary in this situation?

COACHING COMPETENCY BEHAVIORAL MARKER	EVIDENCE FROM COACHING CASE ONE
(continued)	12:00 Yeah. Okay, so you thought about... You've taken some practical steps toward a log, knowing how many hours, thinking about asking to get paid for that, yet something's still holding you back. What do you think that is? 12:00 What's at risk for you if she's annoyed? 14:00 Okay. That side of it is actually fine with you. You have in mind what you want, right? In terms of being some amount. It doesn't matter to me what amount, but you have an amount that would satisfy you for those fifteen hours. That's this month, next month it might be who knows what. You have an amount. You've thought it through in terms of what that amount is, you know the practical steps. What will it take from you to make a move? 21:00 Well, I don't know. I guess the question is, would you want to if you found a way, or is that something you feel like it's satisfying enough for you to see the growth of her business, and you have a piece in that, or will that continue to make you resentful?

COACHING COMPETENCY BEHAVIORAL MARKER	EVIDENCE FROM COACHING CASE ONE
(continued)	22:00 Well, if she was anyone else how would you value it? 23:00 What keeps you from doing that? Just exploring.
3. **Coach's questions help the client explore beyond his/her current thinking to new or expanded ways of thinking about his/her situation.** • Asks the client to look at the situation from different perspectives. • Asks questions that help the client reframe a problem or challenge to a more empowering frame for the client.	5:00 Yeah. Does this sound like anything else that goes on in your life, or is it just this one situation? 16:00 Yeah, I was going to ask you about that. Is there an offer in there somehow? 28:00 In making that request, is there any role in specifying what you'd charge for and what you'd continue to do as a friend, as a coach? 30:00 Okay. What... You said you want to talk to her today before she goes on vacation. Does that still feel like what you want to do? 36:00 Anything else that we should talk about for this situation?

COACHING COMPETENCY BEHAVIORAL MARKER	EVIDENCE FROM COACHING CASE ONE
4. Coach's questions help the client explore beyond current thinking towards the outcome s/he desires. • Asks the client to imagine/picture/articulate her desired future. • Questions help the client create new scenarios that would create success for her goal.	12:00 Okay. What do you want? 14:00 What will it take from you to make a move? 19:00 Is there a loss in there at all for you if you present her with some kind of proposal?
5. Coach asks clear, direct, primarily open-ended questions, one at a time, at a pace that allows for thinking and reflection by the client. • Asks questions that provoke inquiry—questions that cannot be answered literally with a yes or a no. • Allows the client to think before inserting another question.	14:00 What will it take from you to make a move? 25:00 Okay. How'd that feel when you said it out loud?
6. Coach's questions use the client's language and elements of the client's learning style and frame of reference. • Understands and works with the client's learning style (e.g., if client's preferred learning style is by doing, conceptualizing, experimenting, reflecting, visualizing, storytelling, etc.).	6:00 When you get angry about it what happens? 16:00 Is there an offer in there somehow?

COACHING COMPETENCY BEHAVIORAL MARKER	EVIDENCE FROM COACHING CASE ONE
7. Coach's questions are not leading, i.e. do not contain a conclusion or direction.	23:00 What keeps you from doing that? 30:00 Does that still feel like what you want to do?

Case Two Examples

COACHING COMPETENCY BEHAVIORAL MARKER	EVIDENCE FROM COACHING CASE TWO
1. Coach asks questions about the client; his/her way of thinking, assumptions, beliefs, values, needs, wants, etc. • Inquires about thinking, assumptions, beliefs, and values without necessarily using those exact words in the coaching.	3:00 It is in the context within the last sessions of who you want to be as a leader. 6:30 What is your hypothesis of what is going on there? What do you think is coming, that need that people will think like you, do with you? 16:30 Okay so how do you think that this what you're saying affects your leadership? 16:30 How does this affect who you are as a leader?

COACHING COMPETENCY BEHAVIORAL MARKER	EVIDENCE FROM COACHING CASE TWO
2. Coach's questions help the client explore beyond his/her current thinking to new or expanded ways of thinking about himself/herself. • Questions and observations challenge the client's thinking. (Not in all sessions.) • Questions and observations move the client out of the current story she is telling and help her look forward.	8:00 Now that you realize that, now that you have the realization, who would you like to be in this situation as a leader? 9:30 So if you will be a lighthouse and you guide like in the middle for the boat how would that look like and how would you show up as a leader? 15:00 But what does this say about you? 16:00 And that voice, sorry for interrupting you, but that voice was telling you to wait, where do you think it was coming from?
3. Coach's questions help the client explore beyond his/her current thinking to new or expanded ways of thinking about his/her situation. • Asks the client to look at the situation from different perspectives. • Asks questions that help the client reframe a problem or challenge to a more empowering frame for the client.	15:00 What do you think of this scene, if you put a little distance and you look at the scene like a helicopter perspective and you see that, you were talking before, what does this say about them?

COACHING COMPETENCY BEHAVIORAL MARKER	EVIDENCE FROM COACHING CASE TWO
4. Coach's questions help the client explore beyond current thinking towards the outcome s/he desires. • Asks the client to imagine/picture/articulate her desired future. • Questions help the client create new scenarios that would create success for her goal.	18:00 How can you apply these learnings to the question that we have today around building confidence, developing trust in yourself, and being the leader you want to be? 27:00 I am asking you also if you want to consider as a possibility how you can use this not only for your work as a volunteer but also in your personal life. How some conversations came up today about trust, confidence, control can be in some way showing up in other parts of your personal life that you cannot simply take advantage of.
5. Coach asks clear, direct, primarily open-ended questions, one at a time, at a pace that allows for thinking and reflection by the client. • Asks questions that provoke inquiry—questions that cannot be answered literally with a yes or a no. • Allows the client to think before inserting another question.	20:30 And when you are less concerned about that, what is the consequence?

COACHING COMPETENCY BEHAVIORAL MARKER	EVIDENCE FROM COACHING CASE TWO
6. Coach's questions use the client's language and elements of the client's learning style and frame of reference. • Understands and works with the client's learning style (e.g., if client's preferred learning style is by doing, conceptualizing, experimenting, reflecting, visualizing, storytelling, etc.).	23:00 Going back to the metaphor that you used at the beginning of the lighthouse and when you talk about be there and what you're saying now about this trust, like trust and be there, trust in yourself in just being there, and knowing when to participate, not to participate, ready to trust in you, trust in your team how do you think that can translate into steps or actions, something you can do after this session?
7. Coach's questions are not leading, i.e. do not contain a conclusion or direction.	5.00 Okay, so inside of you, around what question would you like to answer or explore? 6:30 What is your hypothesis of what is going on there?

In this chapter, we explored powerful questioning. In the next chapter, we focus on direct communication language and the use of coach interventions that are clear, succinct, and intentional.

FOR FURTHER READING

Merilee Adams, *Change Your Questions, Change Your Life: 10 Powerful Tools for Life and Work* (San Francisco, CA: Berrett-Koehler, 2009).

Tony Stoltzfus, *Coaching Questions: A Coach's Guide to Powerful Asking Skills* (2008), available from http://www.coach22.com.

Laura Whitworth, Karen Kimsey-House, Henry Kimsey-House, and Phillip Sandahl, *Co-Active Coaching: New Skills for Coaching People toward Success in Work and Life* (Boston: Davies Black, 2009).

CHAPTER 7

Direct Communication

> *The ICF defines this competency as the ability "to communicate effectively during coaching sessions, and to use language that has the greatest positive effect on the client."*

D irect communication is one of the three competencies in the "communicating effectively" cluster (along with active listening and powerful questioning). The coach demonstrates this competency when she is clear in the way she communicates, articulates her ideas succinctly, and is direct in providing feedback. To achieve this clarity, the coach must mentally formulate her ideas before sharing them and be intentional in every observation or comment. The ability to summarize and articulate ideas clearly is a skill that needs to be developed in the coach. It requires practice and, above all, a relaxed/present mindset that allows the coach to take her time to think clearly, to explain an idea concisely, or to ask a direct, succinct question.

When the coach is not clear in expressing her ideas, the client may have difficulty understanding. One way to recognize this is when the client asks the coach to repeat what was said or asked. When the coach thinks aloud, it may be difficult for the client to follow her ideas.

BACKGROUND ON DIRECT COMMUNICATION

The coach needs to be clear and careful in expressing her ideas, not only during the session, but also before the coaching engagement starts. By clarifying what coaching is and what the appropriate expectations are for the coaching process, the coach defines a clear agreement. During the coaching process, the coach needs to ensure that the goals for the coaching process, as well as for each session, are succinct so that the journey is focused and effective.

In coaching sessions, less can be more. In other words, talking less and using silence can help the client find her own answers. In a coaching session, the percentage of time the coach talks must be much smaller than the percentage of time the client talks. This competency includes the ability to manage silences. Feeling comfortable with silence, particularly when conducting a session by telephone, is a skill that usually develops with experience. An unexperienced coach may feel the need to say something because she may worry the client will think she doesn't know what to ask or say. In contrast, an experienced coach feels comfortable with silence and understands it as an opportunity for reflection for both herself and the client. Silence is valuable in coaching sessions because it allows reflection and learning. The meaning a coach attributes to silence often makes a difference in how the coaching session progresses.

THE USE OF LANGUAGE

Another key aspect of the direct communication competency is the coach's ability to listen and to use the client's vocabulary during the coaching process. According to the ICF, the coach "uses language appropriate and respectful to the client (e.g., non-sexist, non-racist, non-technical, non-jargon)."

When the coach uses technical language with theoretical distinctions from the coaching school where she trained, the coach is not partnering with the client. To be able to use the vocabulary of the client, you have to pay close attention, and sometimes clarify the meaning the client is giving her words, because they can be different than what you might assume.

For example, when exploring the identity of the client, the coach may ask, "Who are you being in this situation?" The client may not know how to answer that question, because it is not the kind of phrase or question we use in everyday interactions. You may need to further explain the meaning of the question you are asking.

The ability to distinguish assessments from assertions can be very helpful in the work of the coach. Assertions are descriptions of facts that can be measured (like temperature or weight). Assessments are interpretations of the facts and are subjective—they depend on the meaning the "observer" gives to the experience (like cold versus warm, or thin versus fat). By paying attention to language, we may challenge client's interpretations when they believe interpretations are facts (Flores, *Conversations for Action*).

METAPHORS AND ANALOGIES

The coach can use metaphors and analogies to help illustrate an argument or create a verbal picture in the mind of the client (Campbell, *Mining Your Client's Metaphors*). The use of metaphors can be very useful to see the situation from another perspective

(Lawley and Thompkins, *Metaphors in Mind*). In the next examples, we see how the coach uses the client's metaphors to expand an idea for a client. Although in the following examples the metaphor is brought forward by the client, it can be brought by the coach or the client. In this example, notice how this coach works with her client to focus on the metaphor of the whirlwind in her head.

Client: It is such an uncomfortable sensation that I feel, like a literal whirlwind in my head that doesn't let me think. It doesn't let me enjoy the moment. But exactly what other opinions, what else can it be—I do not know. I can't identify it now.

Coach: I'd like to ask your permission to use the metaphor of "whirlwind in the head."

Client: Sure.

Coach: It seems that in the moment you lose effectiveness is when there is a "whirlwind." It can be the moment when you can be very creative, but it also seems to block you, as you have said. So in that moment when you have a "whirlwind in the head," you cannot think clearly.

Client: You know ... while you are telling me this, something is happening to me. Outside of this situation, I have amazing clarity for what I want, and for what I am going to offer. But then it's like all my clarity collapses and I lose coherence and clarity and my emotions become clouded. It's exactly like as you say, yes.

Coach: So to have a different result, would you like to take a moment to visualize this "whirlwind." What is going on?

Client: I visualize it as a tornado that comes and goes. It comes and goes ... and it takes everything.

Coach: What will it take for this tornado ... this whirlwind—that comes into your head to leave so you can have the clarity that you want?

Client: Yes, I am relating to it now. I'm imagining that tornado, like in the movies Tornado or Twister and how to spare the people and prepare them for what is coming. And a little of what I am seeing now, that you're helping me to see, is having the information ready ... having clarity when it will happen, accept that it will happen and be prepared. If I prepare well enough in advance, when the conversation happens, I will be ready and not in a space of suffering.

As the conversation with the client continues, observe as the coach digs deeper into what holds her back in her conversation on service costs with clients.

Client: The truth is that I never asked myself. I rarely dig deep enough to find the answer ... or I do not know if I want to find it.

Coach: So then, the result of selling your services to people may change their opinion about you as a person who values and prioritizes relationships and friendships.

Client: Yes ... yes! And this relates to other situations in which I prefer not to claim what is owed to me, to preserve, and not damage, a relationship or friendship. It is possible that they are linked to each other. This has to do with not wanting to damage my image to maintain that relationship. It's definitely possible. Actually this might be the essential issue, which you've helped raise for me.

MARKERS OF PROFICIENCY IN DIRECT COMMUNICATION

The ICF states that a coach is demonstrating direct communication when there is observable evidence of the following behavioral markers:

1. Coach shares observations, intuitions, comments, thoughts and feelings to serve the client's learning or forward movement.
2. Coach shares observations, intuitions, comments, thoughts and feelings without any attachment to them being right.
3. Coach uses the client's language or language that reflects the client's way of speaking.
4. Coach's language is generally clear and concise.
5. The coach allows the client to do most of the talking.
6. Coach allows the client to complete speaking without interrupting unless there is a stated coaching purpose to do so.

Case One Examples

COACHING COMPETENCY BEHAVIORAL MARKER	EVIDENCE FROM COACHING CASE ONE
1. Coach shares observations, intuitions, comments, thoughts and feelings to serve the client's learning or forward movement. • Coach's statements help the client explore beyond her current thinking to new or expanded ways of thinking. • Coach's statements help the client explore beyond current thinking towards the outcome she desires.	37:00 When you say it now, you seem more confident than you did before. I don't know if you are, but you seem that way.
2. Coach shares observations, intuitions, comments, thoughts and feelings without any attachment to them being right. • Shares beliefs and assessments, not held as truths. • When sharing observations, intuition, comments, thoughts or feelings, coach clearly communicates that they are an "offer" for the client to respond to in any way she chooses.	35:00 Good. That's kind of what I was thinking about is that… Back to your concern that she might offer you something too little, because clearly you got too little for that.

COACHING COMPETENCY BEHAVIORAL MARKER	EVIDENCE FROM COACHING CASE ONE
3. Coach uses the client's language or language that reflects the client's way of speaking. • Uses the client's language as well as introducing new language. • Uses the client's words, speed, speech patterns, etc.	2:00 Yeah. Okay. It's the issue of… I'll play it back and make sure I've got it right. This is a colleague that you've had for a long time. She's now in your building, and you've done a lot of work for her pro bono, it's getting more and more, and it's taking more of your time. She runs a big business, and yet… You haven't charged her, and you're resentful. You kind of want to charge her, but something's holding you back. 28:00 That's really what you're doing, even though you're not nailing down all the specifics today. 10:00 Wow. Yeah, so it really feels unequal now. 11:00 Yeah, so you want to be valued. You want to be valued for the work you do, and value has something to do with finance at this point.
4. Coach's language is generally clear and concise. • When sharing observations, intuitions, comments, thoughts or feelings, coach clearly communicates and articulates in a manner that is easily and readily understood by the client.	8:00 I love that you have that there, and that's one of the ways you calibrate what you do. 9:00 You kind of helped her get to this place, I would guess.

COACHING COMPETENCY BEHAVIORAL MARKER	EVIDENCE FROM COACHING CASE ONE
5. The coach allows the client to do most of the talking. • Talks considerably less than the client (in totality of conversation).	*The transcript shows that the client clearly speaks more. See 1:00, 5:00, 7:00, 8:00, 9:00, 12:00 14:00-16:00, 18:00, 27:00.*
6. Coach allows the client to complete speaking without interrupting unless there is a stated coaching purpose to do so. • If the coach does not interrupt the client during the session, mark the marker. • The coach interrupts only on one or two occasions with a stated coaching purpose. • No interruptions of the client.	*There were no interruptions noted.*

Case Two Examples

COACHING COMPETENCY BEHAVIORAL MARKER	EVIDENCE FROM COACHING CASE TWO
1. **Coach shares observations, intuitions, comments, thoughts and feelings to serve the client's learning or forward movement.** • Coach's statements help the client explore beyond her current thinking to new or expanded ways of thinking. • Coach's statements help the client explore beyond current thinking towards the outcome she desires.	7:00 Even this conversation is not in concrete! 18:00 I heard in this conversation a couple of times where you had some realizations. One when you talk about discovering who you really are as a leader before people have figured out who you are like you knowing yourself. The second one here about the learning about following your heart and from that the relationship and how that affects who you are a leader?
2. **Coach shares observations, intuitions, comments, thoughts and feelings without any attachment to them being right.** • Shares beliefs and assessments, not held as truths. • When sharing observations, intuition, comments, thoughts or feelings, coach clearly communicates that they are an "offer" for the client to respond to in any way she chooses.	18:00 I heard in this conversation a couple of times where you had some realizations. One when you talk about discovering who you really are as a leader before people have figured out who you are like you knowing yourself.

COACHING COMPETENCY BEHAVIORAL MARKER	EVIDENCE FROM COACHING CASE TWO
3. Coach uses the client's language or language that reflects the client's way of speaking. • Uses the client's language as well as introducing new language. • Uses the client's words, speed, speech patterns, etc.	3:00 Trusting you is also related to what you said before about being more confident as a leader.
4. Coach's language is generally clear and concise. • When sharing observations, intuitions, comments, thoughts or feelings, coach clearly communicates and articulates in a manner that is easily and readily understood by the client.	3:00 It is in the context within the last sessions of who you want to be as a leader. 21:00 What you're saying is it's about trusting people. Is that it? That you're trusting people even without seeing them. 27:30 I am asking you also if you want to consider as a possibility how you can use this not only for your work as a volunteer but also in your personal life.
5. The coach allows the client to do most of the talking. • Talks considerably less than the client (in totality of conversation).	*During the session, the client did most of the talking. Specific examples in the transcript are at 1:00, 3:30, 5:30, 7:30, 8:30, 10:30–14:30, 18:30, and 23:30–25:30.*

COACHING COMPETENCY BEHAVIORAL MARKER	EVIDENCE FROM COACHING CASE TWO
6. Coach allows the client to complete speaking without interrupting unless there is a stated coaching purpose to do so. • If the coach does not interrupt the client during the session, mark the marker. • The coach interrupts only on one or two occasions with a stated coaching purpose. • No interruptions of the client.	*The coach interrupted the client at 16:00. This interruption had a coaching purpose.* And that voice, sorry for interrupting you, but that voice was telling you to wait. Where do you think it was coming from? *Otherwise no interruptions were noted.*

In this chapter, we discussed direct communication. In our next chapter, we focus on creating awareness and how the coach encourages the client to explore her learning from multiple perspectives.

FOR FURTHER READING

Gina Campbell, *Mining your Client's Metaphors: A How-To Workbook on Clean Language and Symbolic Modeling* (Bloomington, IN: Balboa Press, 2013).

Fernando Flores, *Conversations for Action and Collected Essays: Instilling a Culture of Commitment in Working Relationships* (Createspace, 2012).

James Lawley and Penny Tompkins, *Metaphors in Mind: Transformation through Symbolic Modeling* (London: The Development Company, 2000).

Part Four:
Facilitating Learning
and Results

Creating Awareness

> The ICF defines this competency as the ability "to integrate and accurately evaluate multiple sources of information, and to make interpretations that help the client to gain awareness and thereby achieve agreed-upon results."

There are four competencies that come together to comprise the fourth cluster, which focuses on "facilitating learning and results": creating awareness, designing actions, planning and defining objectives, and fostering progress and accountability.

BACKGROUND ON CREATING AWARENESS

According to the ICF, a coach demonstrates the ability to create awareness when she "goes beyond what is said in assessing client's concerns, not getting hooked by the client's description." If coaches limit their analysis to address only what clients say, they will not be able to explore underlying issues, and sessions are likely to remain at a superficial level, limiting the potential for advancement or true progress. For example, if the client wants to work on being more punctual, and the coach chooses to focus solely on the importance of being on time and brainstorms ideas on how to be on time, she may miss the opportunity to discover deeper and more influential issues, such as the personal costs and benefits of being late or other unseen factors that might underlie a pattern.

To create awareness, we need to allow the client to see new opportunities for action from a different perspective. From an ontological coaching perspective, creating awareness means producing a change in the client as an "observer" of her reality (see Fernando Flores, *Conversations for Action*). A beginner coach is capable of working at a superficial level that corresponds to the first-degree learning style of "observer-action-solution" (see Chalmers Brothers, *Language and the Pursuit of Happiness*). Although different actions do lead to different results, the change may be superficial. In contrast, an experienced coach may be able to explore what the client says in a deeper manner, clarifying beliefs, values, assumptions, and fears that can get in the way of getting results. This deeper exploration allows a change to occur in the way the client interprets reality. There is a change in the "observer," who, in turn, designs new actions and achieves results that can be applied not only to the concrete situation in question, but also to other areas of life as well.

EXAMPLES OF CREATING AWARENESS

The following session demonstrates an example of this deeper exploration approach:

Coach: It seems that you now have something specific and concrete that you can do in relation to the goals from our working agreement for the session. We talked about *what* you are going to do; my question now is *who* are you going to be when doing these things?

We can clearly see how the coach moves from a "what to do" level of inquiry to a "who am I" level of introspection, and thus begins to conduct a more profound, and potentially much more powerful exploration. The coach is now coaching the *who* of the client and not just the *what* of the situation.

Client: What a great question! [A common client response following a coach's powerful question.] Who will I be in these situations is something I have never asked myself, at least not until now. I think I can be someone with more confidence, someone who understands that a relationship will not necessarily be harmed by me clearly asserting my needs, and I think if people are coming to me to hire me, it is because they see the value of my work, and it is not a sin for me to charge a fee for that work. I make my living and my family's living from that fee, and if I don't insist on being paid, it will affect not only me, but my family as well. I think I need to identify it, to have it be clear, and to be able to be someone who has the clarity to feel comfortable saying what I believe needs to be said.

Coach: Then it is not only about what you would do, or how you would be prepared for a given situation, but also about who you will be in that situation. What I am hearing you say is that you would be someone who is more confident, someone who knows they have something valuable to offer and who has responsibilities to his family, and deserves to be compensated for the work that he performs.

Client: Yes, I agree.

Coach: Therefore, if you are going to be this confident, responsible, committed person, not only with the value you offer but also in your personal relationships, what other possibilities open up? [The coach checks for a change in the observer.]

Client: The possibility of enjoying these experiences instead of feeling I am providing a service to friends for a lower pay because of a personal relationship. I might stop resenting them for paying less than I am worth. But if I feel that there is value in what I'm offering, it will not negatively affect the relationship. I have decided to work and support my family. I think I can enjoy it by knowing this.

CREATING AWARENESS IN THE COACHING PROCESS

The coach "invokes inquiry for greater understanding, awareness, and clarity." Asking powerful questions helps the client to investigate her own issues and to work and analyze new perspectives and viewpoints. Many times, it is in the act of answering a coach's questions that a client reaches clarity, primarily because of the need to structure her ideas when formulating a response. This can be of great value and can help a client develop greater clarity to make decisions so she will be more effective in reaching her goals. The process of thinking out loud and being able to structure ideas creates awareness, sometimes without much participation from the coach.

The coach "identifies for the client his/her underlying concerns, typical and fixed ways of perceiving himself/herself and the world, differences between the facts and the interpretation, disparities between thoughts, feelings and action." The coach pays close attention to the client's discourse and applies active listening skills, going beyond what is said and paying attention to what is expressed by body language and even silence.

A distinction that the coach can introduce and incorporate into her work with the client is the distinction between situations and the interpretation of those situations. When the client realizes that her interpretations belong to her and not to the situation, the potential develops for a new outlook and, further, new possibilities of action to obtain results.

The coach "helps clients to discover for themselves the new thoughts, beliefs, perceptions, emotions, moods, etc., that strengthen their ability to take action and achieve what is important to them." With powerful questioning and active listening, the coach opens up a space for reflection, allowing new possibilities for action. The coach differentiates between "what I know I know," "what I know I do not know," and "what I don't know that I don't know." This awareness can create an opening for the client, providing her amplified focus or a different perspective on a situation.

The coach "helps clients to see the different, interrelated factors that affect them and their behaviors (e.g., thoughts, emotions, body, background)." During the exploration of these variables, the client may realize that there are other factors that have not been considered, and may be discoverable with a new perspective of what is or is not working.

Here is another example with a different client:

Coach: What is possible for you now as a result of this conversation? [This is a way to check to see whether there were any changes in the client's perspective and whether the objective was reached.]

Client: I can tell that the insecurity that I feel has nothing to do with anything that is happening to me right now, but rather something from the past. You could call it something like the impostor's syndrome. I know I can't resolve this old conflict now. I will not only resolve the one problem that I have relating to this seminar, but also I will be resolving an obstacle that I have in being able to expose myself and take risks in other situations.

When there is this kind of change in the observer, the effects are clear to see. The newfound effectiveness that the change brings is not limited to just one area, but affects other areas of a client's life as well.

Client: I also realize now that one of my biggest fears has been that I do not know enough and that I am not successful just as I am. When you repeatedly asked me to think about myself, I saw a mirror in which I was able to see what I did not notice before. I recognized, and was aware on some level, but was not able to ask the question of myself.

The client is referring to the coach's "who will you be" question. She appreciated the role of the coach as mirror, along with the effects of the coach's interventions. By pointing to *who* she is going to *be* instead of to *what* she is going to *do*, the client experiences a change in her perspectives before designing any actions.

The coach identifies the main points and areas of learning and growth in the client, as well as what she believes requires priority attention during the coaching process. Many executives who work with coaches to improve areas of weakness in preparation for future challenges create development plans that identify areas of weakness, as well as strengths. These plans work as guides for the coaching, and sometimes as documents that companies request as proof that the coaching is beneficial.

When the coach detects a weakness that is consistent with what the client says and what she does, the coach can attempt to act as the client's mirror. In this way, the coach can help the client differentiate between perceived and actual behaviors.

The observations presented by the coach require client validation. An opportunity should be provided for the client to express her own observations and reactions to what the coach says. In summary, the coach helps the client get involved in a process of analysis, learning, and discovery.

MARKERS OF PROFICIENCY IN CREATING AWARENESS

The ICF states that a coach is demonstrating competency in creating awareness when there is observable evidence of the following behavioral markers:

1. Coach invites client to state and/or explore his/her learning in the session about her/his situation (the *what*).
2. Coach invites client to state and/or explore his/her learning in the session about her/himself (the *who*).
3. Coach shares what s/he is noticing about the client and/or the client's situation, and seeks the client's input or exploration.
4. Coach invites client to consider how s/he will use new learning from the coaching.

5. Coach's questions, intuitions and observations have the potential to create new learning for the client.

Case One Examples

COACHING COMPETENCY BEHAVIORAL MARKER	EVIDENCE FROM COACHING CASE ONE
1. **Coach invites client to state and/or explore his/her learning in the session about her/his situation (the *what*).** • Asks about insights, learnings, and take-aways during and/or at end of session.	37:00 What learnings did you have from the session? 37:00 Will you let me know the resolution?
2. **Coach invites client to state and/or explore his/her learning in the session about her/himself (the *who*).** • Inquires how new awareness/learning influences the client's behavior or way of being in the situation or perceiving herself.	12:00 You've taken some practical steps toward a log, knowing how many hours, thinking about asking to get paid for that, yet something's still holding you back. What do you think that is? 37:00 What learnings did you have from the session?

COACHING COMPETENCY BEHAVIORAL MARKER	EVIDENCE FROM COACHING CASE ONE
3. Coach shares what s/he is noticing about the client and/or the client's situation, and seeks the client's input or exploration. • As evidenced by coach inquiring about or noticing the client's emotions, body language, tone of voice, patterns of thought, and patterns of language.	10:00 Wow. Yeah, so it really feels unequal now. 12:00 Yeah. Okay, so you thought about... You've taken some practical steps toward a log, knowing how many hours, thinking about asking to get paid for that, yet something's still holding you back. What do you think that is? 13:00 Okay. If that were to happen, if she were to say, "No." Hire somebody else or thank you, or... What would... ? 16:00 Yeah, I was going to ask you about that. Is there an offer in there somehow? 20:00 Yeah. I'm kind of hearing, if I can play back this to you. I'm kind of hearing three buckets, and I don't know, tell me if that's what you mean, because maybe those offers are different for different buckets. One bucket is HR work, right? That bucket, it sounds like you don't have any ambivalence at all about counting up the number of hours and asking for a reasonable amount of pay. Would that be right? 22:00 That hasn't happened. Again, I don't know, are those the three buckets, or is there something else?

COACHING COMPETENCY BEHAVIORAL MARKER	EVIDENCE FROM COACHING CASE ONE
4. Coach invites client to consider how s/he will use new learning from the coaching. • States or links the client's new learning to the client's session or meta-goal, as a result of the coaching session process. • Invites the client to broaden the impact of learning to other situations or ways of being.	5:00 Does this sound like anything else that goes on in your life or is it just this one situation? 13:00 If that were to happen, if she were to say, "No." Hire somebody else or thank you. What would your response be?
5. Coach's questions, intuitions and observations have the potential to create new learning for the client. • Coach asks permission to consult, teach or mentor occasionally when in service of the client's immediate or longer-term agenda. • Coach's sharing of her own ideas, options, intuition or wisdom has the potential to expand the client's awareness and choice points or advance the client's agenda.	9:00 You kind of helped her get to this place, I would guess. 11:00 So you want to be valued for the work you do, and value has something to do with finance at this point?

Case Two Examples

COACHING COMPETENCY BEHAVIORAL MARKER	EVIDENCE FROM COACHING CASE TWO
1. Coach invites client to state and/or explore his/her learning in the session about her/his situation (the *what*). • Asks about insights, learnings, and take-aways during and/or at end of session	22:00 Based on our conversation and what you wanted to accomplish in this session, where are you?
2. Coach invites client to state and/or explore his/her learning in the session about her/himself (the *who*). • Inquires how new awareness/learning influences the client's behavior or way of being in the situation or perceiving herself.	9:30 So if you will be a lighthouse and you guide like in the middle for the boat how would that look like and how would you show up as a leader? 16:00 What happened when this was coming from your heart different than from your head? 20:30 And when you are less concerned about that, what is the consequence?

COACHING COMPETENCY BEHAVIORAL MARKER	EVIDENCE FROM COACHING CASE TWO
3. Coach shares what s/he is noticing about the client and/or the client's situation, and seeks the client's input or exploration. • As evidenced by coach inquiring about or noticing the client's emotions, body language, tone of voice, patterns of thought, and patterns of language.	18:00 I heard in this conversation a couple of times where you had some realizations. One when you talk about discovering who you really are as a leader before people have figured out who you are like you knowing yourself. The second one here about the learning about following your heart and from that the relationship and how that affect who you are a leader? How can you apply these learnings to the question that we have today around building confidence, developing trust in yourself, and being the leader you want to be?
4. Coach invites client to consider how s/he will use new learning from the coaching. • States or links the client's new learning to the client's session or meta-goal, as a result of the coaching session process. • Invites the client to broaden the impact of learning to other situations or ways of being.	23:00 Going back to the metaphor that you used at the beginning of the lighthouse and when you talk about be there and what you're saying now about this trust, like trust and be there, trust in yourself in just being there, and knowing when to participate, not to participate, ready to trust in you, trust in your team how do you think that can translate into steps or actions, something you can do after this session?

COACHING COMPETENCY BEHAVIORAL MARKER	EVIDENCE FROM COACHING CASE TWO
5. Coach's questions, intuitions and observations have the potential to create new learning for the client. • Coach asks permission to consult, teach or mentor occasionally when in service of the client's immediate or longer-term agenda. • Coach's sharing of her own ideas, options, intuition or wisdom has the potential to expand the client's awareness and choice points or advance the client's agenda.	21:30 What you're saying is it's about trusting people, is that it? That you're trusting people even without seeing them. 17:30 I heard in this conversation a couple of times where you had some realizations. How can you apply these learnings to the question that we have today around building confidence?

Throughout this chapter, several examples and suggestions are given to help coaches create awareness in their clients. The next chapter will build on facilitating learning and results as we explore the role of designing actions, planning and goal setting, and managing progress and accountability.

FOR FURTHER READING

W. Chalmers Brothers, Jr., *Language and the Pursuit of Happiness: A New Foundation for Designing Your Life, Your Relationships & Your Results* (Naples, FL: New Possibilities Press, 2005).

Fernando Flores, *Conversations for Action and Collected Essays: Instilling a Culture of Commitment in Working Relationships* (Createspace, 2012).

Judith Wilson and Michelle Gislason, *Coaching Skills for Nonprofit Managers and Leaders: Developing People to Achieve Your Mission* (San Francisco, CA: Jossey-Bass, 2010).

Designing Actions / Planning and Goal Setting / Managing Progress and Accountability

> *The ICF defines these competencies as the ability "to create with the client opportunities for ongoing learning, during coaching and in work/life situations, and for taking new actions that will most effectively lead to agreed-upon coaching results"; the ability "to develop and maintain an effective coaching plan with the client"; and the ability "to hold attention on what is important for the client, and to leave responsibility with the client to take action," respectively.*

These three competencies are part of the cluster on "facilitating learning and results." They are assessed together, and there is only one set of behavioral markers for all three competencies.

BACKGROUND ON DESIGNING ACTIONS, GOAL SETTING, AND MANAGING PROGRESS AND ACCOUNTABILITY

The coach explores the client's concerns or goals throughout the session, and as a result of the powerful questioning, the coach supports the client to become more conscious about the issue and to see the situation from a different perspective. However, if the process does not go beyond the exploration-and-insight stage, the coaching may not be very effective. It is important for that insight to be translated into specific actions that were not available to the client at the beginning of the session, before the exploration. In some situations, the client needs to keep thinking and "digesting" what she learned in the session before moving to actions. The coach needs to meet the client wherever she is. Designing actions may not be urgent, but the coach is expected to offer this option to the client. For example, the coach may ask, "What would you like to do with your learning from this session?"

Part of the coach's responsibility is to work with the client to find actions that will allow her to achieve what was agreed on at the beginning of the session. It is not about jumping to problem solving, brainstorming, and taking immediate action, but, rather, allowing the client to explore what she might want to achieve in the session to work toward her goal. If we try to identify possible actions from the beginning of the session, the client might come out satisfied with the conversation and with many actions to take, but with superficial and limited knowledge about herself, her beliefs, her blind spots and blocks. She will not benefit as much in her "whole" life.

By asking powerful questions, the coach partners with the client to explore the client's concerns, and the result of that exploration is the opportunity to implement what was learned during the session.

The coach knows it is not enough to leave the client with the first alternatives; instead, she works with the client to identify alternatives, perhaps beyond what she thinks is possible, to achieve her goal. Sometimes it is good to brainstorm to select possible actions, without filtering for any judgments the client might have of the ideas. Instead, the coach and client partner to evaluate each idea to decide which are most realistic and appropriate after the creative process. Barriers to achieving the goal should also be explored, along with potential support mechanisms for goal achievement.

Ideally, the client should always identify her own actions. If the coach proposes actions, she should be careful to avoid falling into the role of expert or consultant (see Mary Beth O'Neill's *Executive Coaching with Backbone and Heart*). After the client explores her own ideas to accomplish her goals, an effective coach may propose activities that imply challenges for the client. This provides a more productive learning experience. If the client only identifies actions to work on that are at her comfort level, it is useful for the coach to explore new activities that imply new methods to take risks. This may be uncomfortable for the client but it may also produce more meaningful learning and results. If the coach has specific training in the area she is working in with the client, or if she knows of clients that benefited from the determined activities, the coach can recommend actions—but as possibilities, without having the client feel forced to practice the recommended actions and without being attached to the client's acceptance of her suggestions.

Increased self-awareness discussed in the previous chapter ultimately may help us identify new potential actions. To create consciousness, new behaviors are identified, and this implies risk on the part of the client. During the self-discovery phase, the client can notice her self-imposed barriers. Alternatively, the client might notice that there are new abilities that need to be developed if she wants to achieve new results.

The capacity for self-discovery can depend on the person's emotional intelligence, past work on herself such as therapy, previous coaching experiences, participation in personal discovery workshops, reading self-help books, and other life experiences. These may bring self-knowledge and self-awareness about her strengths and weaknesses. Also, it is relative to the person's willingness and commitment to learn and grow in new areas. There are people who have low motivation for self-discovery and are not open to learning more about themselves. In these cases, the work of the coach can focus on having the client feel comfortable in this area before beginning to identify a course of action.

The coach can challenge the client's point of view as an opportunity to learn and to motivate the client to consider new perspectives. Although it can be uncomfortable, it can help the client reevaluate her concerns. By learning about new perspectives, the client can take actions that were not accessible before the conversation. Some people have trouble exploring new perspectives and may be at different levels of "readiness" to work on themselves to produce results (see Peter Bluckert's *Psychological Dimensions of Executive Coaching*). This may have to do with their insecurities because they fear the unknown or the uncertainty. It is important to explore the client's reluctance, because this may interfere with her progress and success.

An experienced coach knows that for a client to see results, she usually needs specific deadlines and concrete activities. If specific dates are not agreed on, it is more difficult to have follow-up. Asking the client about obstacles to implementing the plan can be useful. The coach or the client might have a very interesting course of action, but if there is no consideration of the obstacles, the plan may just stay on paper. The analysis of obstacles can be key to implementing the plan, because it allows the client to be ready to face them (see Foster and Auerbach's *Positive Psychology in Coaching: Applying Science to Executive and Personal Coaching;* and Wilson and Gislason's *Coaching Skills for Nonprofit Managers and Leaders*).

This group of competencies is intended to create learning opportunities during each coaching session for the client in her work and life. It is about working with the client to plan activities that can be completed outside the sessions, to continue exploring, to be more conscious, and to move toward a desired objective.

As mentioned in previous chapters, the partnering between coach and client is evident in the use of these competencies. Coach and client should partner to close the coaching session so that it does not have an abrupt ending. As mentioned in the discussion of creating trust and intimacy, noticing and reflecting the client's progress in the session is important in managing accountability and can be especially important at the end of the session. The client hears support from the coach that may enhance her ability to carry forward the agreed-on actions when the session is finished.

MARKERS OF PROFICIENCY IN DESIGNING ACTIONS, PLANNING AND GOAL SETTING, AND MANAGING PROGRESS AND ACCOUNTABILITY

For the purposes of evaluating a coaching session, the ICF has grouped these three competencies together. The ICF states that a coach is demonstrating the competencies of designing actions, planning and goal setting, and managing progress and accountability when there is observable evidence of the following behavioral markers:

1. Coach invites or allows client to explore progress towards what s/he wants to accomplish in the session.

2. Coach assists the client to design what actions/thinking the client will do after the session in order for the client to continue moving toward the client's desired outcomes.

3. Coach invites or allows client to consider her/his path forward, including, as appropriate, support mechanisms, resources and potential barriers.

4. Coach assists the client to design the best methods of accountability for her/himself.

5. Coach partners with the client to close the session.

6. Coach notices and reflects client's progress.

Case One Examples

COACHING COMPETENCY BEHAVIORAL MARKER	EVIDENCE FROM COACHING CASE ONE
1. Coach invites or allows client to explore progress towards what s/he wants to accomplish in the session. • Inquires about the client's progress toward the goal. • Follows up on the client's stated progress, or lack of progress, toward the goal.	24:00 Where are you now with those strategies? Let's just check in.

COACHING COMPETENCY BEHAVIORAL MARKER	EVIDENCE FROM COACHING CASE ONE
2. Coach assists the client to design what actions/thinking client will do after the session in order for the client to continue moving toward the client's desired outcomes. • Actions may look like: further thinking; additional feeling or living with an idea; self-inquiry; behavior change; task completion; research; or experimentation.	26:00 Is there anything else you have to resolve in yourself before you go into that conversation? 31:00 What will help you make sure that ball doesn't drop? 33:00 I wonder about the time she's on vacation, how you might use that to firm up your request or your offer. 36:00 In what way might you have to prepare for that subsequent conversation. 36:00 Anything else that we should talk about for this situation?
3. Coach invites or allows client to consider her/his path forward, including, as appropriate, support mechanisms, resources and potential barriers. • Explores likelihood of an action to occur in the future (e.g. use of a scaling question). • Inquires about the client's feeling about the action. • Tests the client's level of willingness to execute.	31:00 I'm wondering what will make sure... What will help you make sure that ball doesn't drop? Because it might be uncomfortable when she gets back. 31:00 I don't doubt your calendar. I'm questioning your resolve. 36:00 Not only putting it on your calendar, but in what way you might have to prepare for that subsequent conversation.

COACHING COMPETENCY BEHAVIORAL MARKER	EVIDENCE FROM COACHING CASE ONE
4. Coach assists the client to design the best methods of accountability for her/himself. • Coach can serve as an accountability partner on occasion. • Inquires about other forms of support for client accountability structures.	32:00 is there anything else about this that will help you get to the resolution that you want? 37:00 Will you let me know the resolution?
5. Coach partners with the client to close the session. • Invites the client to consider how she wants to complete the session. • Checks in with the client on what topics the client is complete with and what may need to be carried to work on outside the session or in the next session.	32:00 As we finish up then, is there anything else about this that will help you get to the resolution that you want? 36:00 Anything else that we should talk about for this situation? I know it'll be hard, but I'll be rooting here for you. 39:00 Is there something you wished would've happened that didn't? An area I could've explored but I didn't?
6. Coach notices and reflects client's progress. • Celebrates the client's success when the client executes on agreed action commitments. • Inquires about obstacles that got in the way of the client's efforts to follow through on actions.	8:00 I love that you have that there. 24:00 Yeah, that's what makes you a good coach. 31:00 That's a big step for you.

Case Two Examples

COACHING COMPETENCY BEHAVIORAL MARKER	EVIDENCE FROM COACHING CASE TWO
1. Coach invites or allows client to explore progress towards what s/he want to accomplish in the session. • Inquires about the client's progress toward the goal. • Follows up on the client's stated progress, or lack of progress, toward the goal.	22:00 We need to start wrapping up. Based on our conversation and what you wanted to accomplish in this session, where are you?
2. Coach assists the client to design what actions/thinking client will do after the session in order for the client to continue moving toward the client's desired outcomes. • Actions may look like: further thinking; additional feeling or living with an idea; self-inquiry; behavior change; task completion; research; or experimentation.	23:30 How do you think that can translate into steps or actions, something you can do after this session?

COACHING COMPETENCY BEHAVIORAL MARKER	EVIDENCE FROM COACHING CASE TWO
3. **Coach invites or allows client to consider her/his path forward, including, as appropriate, support mechanisms, resources and potential barriers.** • Explores likelihood of an action to occur in the future (e.g. use of a scaling question). • Inquires about the client's feeling about the action. • Tests the client's level of willingness to execute.	18:00 I heard in this conversation a couple of times where you had some realizations. One when you talk about discovering who you really are as a leader before people have figured out who you are like you knowing yourself. The second one here about the learning about following your heart and from that the relationship and how that affect who you are a leader? How can you apply these learnings to the question that we have today around building confidence, developing trust in yourself, and being the leader you want to be?
4. **Coach assists the client to design the best methods of accountability for her/himself.** • Coach can serve as an accountability partner on occasion. • Inquires about other forms of support for client accountability structures.	*Not demonstrated*
5. **Coach partners with the client to close the session.** • Invites the client to consider how she wants to complete the session. • Checks in with the client on what topics the client is complete with and what.	26:30 Okay, how do you want to wrap up this session today?

COACHING COMPETENCY BEHAVIORAL MARKER	EVIDENCE FROM COACHING CASE TWO
6. Coach notices and reflects client's progress. • Celebrates the client's success when the client executes on agreed action commitments. • Inquires about obstacles that got in the way of the client's efforts to follow through on actions.	26:00 Just to make a comment, so when you're asking questions you said a couple of things that I wanted to bring to your attention. When you ask questions and when you're working with people and delegating activities you see you're going to be trusting them. So it seems that you may bring consciously your belief that they can be trusted and you are choosing to trust them. And at the same time you are going to support them so I want to be supportive I want to be able to think I will be there and at the same time be more comfortable in delegating tasks to other people.

In this chapter, we tied together the final three competencies, designing actions, planning and goal setting, and managing progress and accountability. These competencies are well-integrated with each other and are an outgrowth of the earlier eight competencies. In the appendix, you will read two complete coaching session transcripts in their entirety where we have highlighted the corresponding coaching competencies, and the coaching competency behavioral markers, for your review.

FOR FURTHER READING

Peter Bluckert, *Psychological Dimensions of Executive Coaching* (Maidenhead: Open University Press, 2006).

Mary Beth A. O'Neil, *Executive Coaching with Backbone and Heart: A Systems Approach to Engaging Leaders with Their Challenges* (San Francisco, CA: Jossey-Bass, 2013).

Judith Wilson and Michelle Gislason, *Coaching Skills for Nonprofit Managers and Leaders: Developing People to Achieve Your Mission* (San Francisco, CA: Jossey-Bass, 2010).

Sandra Foster and Jeffrey Auerbach, *Positive Psychology in Coaching* (Arroyo Grande, CA: Executive College Press, 2015).

The ICF Professional Certified Coach Markers

Reprinted With Permission From The International Coach Federation

Assessment markers are the indicators that an assessor is trained to listen for to determine which ICF Core Competencies are in evidence in a recorded coaching conversation, and to what extent. The following markers are the behaviors that should be exhibited in a coaching conversation at the Professional Certified Coach (PCC) level. These markers support a performance evaluation process that is fair, consistent, valid, reliable, repeatable and defensible. Please note these markers are not a tool for coaching, and should not be used as a checklist or formula for passing the performance evaluation.

Competency 2: Creating the Coaching Agreement

- Coach helps the client identify, or reconfirm, what s/he wants to accomplish in the session.
- Coach helps the client to define or reconfirm measures of success for what s/he wants to accomplish in the session.
- Coach explores what is important or meaningful to the client about what s/he wants to accomplish in the session.
- Coach helps the client define what the client believes he/she needs to address or resolve in order to achieve what s/he wants to accomplish in the session.

- Coach continues conversation in direction of client's desired outcome unless client indicates otherwise.

Competency 3: Creating Trust and Intimacy

- Coach acknowledges and respects the client's work in the coaching process.
- Coach expresses support for the client.
- Coach encourages and allows the client to fully express him/herself.

Competency 4: Coaching Presence

- Coach acts in response to both the whole person of the client and what the client wants to accomplish in the session.
- Coach is observant, empathetic, and responsive.
- Coach notices and explores energy shifts in the client.
- Coach exhibits curiosity with the intent to learn more.
- Coach partners with the client by supporting the client to choose what happens in the session.
- Coach partners with the client by inviting the client to respond in any way to the coach's contributions and accepts the client's response.
- Coach partners with the client by playing back the client's expressed possibilities for the client to choose from.
- Coach partners with the client by encouraging the client to formulate his or her own learning.

Competency 5: Active Listening

- Coach's questions and observations are customized by using what the coach has learned about who the client is and the client's situation.

- Coach inquires about or explores the client's use of language.
- Coach inquires about or explores the client's emotions.
- Coach inquires about or explores the client's tone of voice, pace of speech or inflection as appropriate.
- Coach inquires about or explores the client's behaviors.
- Coach inquires about or explores how the client perceives his/her world.
- Coach is quiet and gives client time to think.

Competency 6: Powerful Questioning

- Coach asks questions about the client; his/her way of thinking, assumptions, beliefs, values, needs, wants, etc.
- Coach's questions help the client explore beyond his/her current thinking to new or expanded ways of thinking about himself/herself.
- Coach's questions help the client explore beyond his/her current thinking to new or expanded ways of thinking about his/her situation.
- Coach's questions help the client explore beyond current thinking towards the outcome s/he desires.
- Coach asks clear, direct, primarily open-ended questions, one at a time, at a pace that allows for thinking and reflection by the client.
- Coach's questions use the client's language and elements of the client's learning style and frame of reference.
- Coach's questions are not leading, i.e. do not contain a conclusion or direction.

Competency 7: Direct Communication

- Coach shares observations, intuitions, comments, thoughts and feelings to serve the client's learning or forward movement.
- Coach shares observations, intuitions, comments, thoughts and feelings without any attachment to them being right.
- Coach uses the client's language or language that reflects the client's way of speaking.
- Coach's language is generally clear and concise.
- The coach allows the client to do most of the talking.
- Coach allows the client to complete speaking without interrupting unless there is a stated coaching purpose to do so.

Competency 8: Creating Awareness

- Coach invites client to state and/or explore his/her learning in the session about her/his situation (the what).
- Coach invites client to state and/or explore his/her learning in the session about her-/himself (the who).
- Coach shares what s/he is noticing about the client and / or the client's situation, and seeks the client's input or exploration.
- Coach invites client to consider how s/he will use new learning from the coaching.
- Coach's questions, intuitions and observations have the potential to create new learning for the client.

Competency 9, 10 and 11: Designing Actions, Planning and Goal Setting, and Managing Progress and Accountability

- Coach invites or allows client to explore progress towards what s/he want to accomplish in the session.

- Coach assists the client to design what actions/thinking client will do after the session in order for the client to continue moving toward the client's desired outcomes.
- Coach invites or allows client to consider her/his path forward, including, as appropriate, support mechanisms, resources and potential barriers.
- Coach assists the client to design the best methods of accountability for her/himself.
- Coach partners with the client to close the session.
- Coach notices and reflects client's progress.

Code of Ethics of the International Coach Federation

Reprinted With Permission From The International Coach Federation

I CF is committed to maintaining and promoting excellence in coaching. Therefore, ICF expects all members and credentialed coaches (coaches, coach mentors, coaching supervisors, coach trainers or students), to adhere to the elements and principles of ethical conduct: to be competent and integrate ICF Core Competencies effectively in their work.

In line with the ICF core values and ICF definition of coaching, the Code of Ethics is designed to provide appropriate guidelines, accountability and enforceable standards of conduct for all ICF Members and ICF Credential-holders, who commit to abiding by the following ICF Code of Ethics:

PART ONE: DEFINITIONS

- **COACHING:** Coaching is partnering with clients in a thought-provoking and creative process that inspires them to maximize their personal and professional potential.
- **ICF COACH:** An ICF coach agrees to practice the ICF Core Competencies and pledges accountability to the ICF Code of Ethics.
- **PROFESSIONAL COACHING RELATIONSHIP:** A professional coaching relationship exists when coaching includes

an agreement (including contracts) that defines the responsibilities of each party.

- **ROLES IN THE COACHING RELATIONSHIP:** In order to clarify roles in the coaching relationship it is often necessary to distinguish between the client and the sponsor. In most cases, the client and sponsor are the same person and are therefore jointly referred to as the client. For purposes of identification, however, the ICF defines these roles as follows:
- **CLIENT:** The "Client/Coachee" is the person(s) being coached.
- **SPONSOR:** The "sponsor" is the entity (including its representatives) paying for and/or arranging for coaching services to be provided. In all cases, coaching engagement agreements should clearly establish the rights, roles and responsibilities for both the client and sponsor if the client and sponsor are different people.
- **STUDENT:** The "student" is someone enrolled in a coach training program or working with a coaching supervisor or coach mentor in order to learn the coaching process or enhance and develop their coaching skills.
- **CONFLICT OF INTEREST:** A situation in which a coach has a private or personal interest sufficient to appear to influence the objective of his or her official duties as a coach and a professional.

PART TWO: THE ICF STANDARDS OF ETHICAL CONDUCT

Section 1: Professional Conduct at Large

As a coach, I:

1. Conduct myself in accordance with the ICF Code of Ethics in all interactions, including coach training, coach mentoring and coach supervisory activities.

2. Commit to take the appropriate action with the coach, trainer, or coach mentor and/or will contact ICF to address any ethics violation or possible breach as soon as I become aware, whether it involves me or others.

3. Communicate and create awareness in others, including organizations, employees, sponsors, coaches and others, who might need to be informed of the responsibilities established by this Code.

4. Refrain from unlawful discrimination in occupational activities, including age, race, gender orientation, ethnicity, sexual orientation, religion, national origin or disability.

5. Make verbal and written statements that are true and accurate about what I offer as a coach, the coaching profession or ICF.

6. Accurately identify my coaching qualifications, expertise, experience, training, certifications and ICF Credentials.

7. Recognize and honor the efforts and contributions of others and only claim ownership of my own material. I understand that violating this standard may leave me subject to legal remedy by a third party.

8. Strive at all times to recognize my personal issues that may impair, conflict with or interfere with my coaching performance or my professional coaching relationships. I will

promptly seek the relevant professional assistance and determine the action to be taken, including whether it is appropriate to suspend or terminate my coaching relationship(s) whenever the facts and circumstances necessitate.

9. Recognize that the Code of Ethics applies to my relationship with coaching clients, coachees, students, mentees and supervisees.

10. Conduct and report research with competence, honesty and within recognized scientific standards and applicable subject guidelines. My research will be carried out with the necessary consent and approval of those involved, and with an approach that will protect participants from any potential harm. All research efforts will be performed in a manner that complies with all the applicable laws of the country in which the research is conducted.

11. Maintain, store and dispose of any records, including electronic files and communications, created during my coaching engagements in a manner that promotes confidentiality, security and privacy and complies with any applicable laws and agreements.

12. Use ICF Member contact information (email addresses, telephone numbers, and so on) only in the manner and to the extent authorized by the ICF.

Section 2: Conflicts of Interest

As a coach, I:

13. Seek to be conscious of any conflict or potential conflict of interest, openly disclose any such conflict and offer to remove myself when a conflict arises.

14. Clarify roles for internal coaches, set boundaries and review with stakeholders conflicts of interest that may emerge between coaching and other role functions.
15. Disclose to my client and the sponsor(s) all anticipated compensation from third parties that I may receive for referrals of clients or pay to receive clients.
16. Honor an equitable coach/client relationship, regardless of the form of compensation.

Section 3: Professional Conduct with Clients

As a coach, I:

17. Ethically speak what I know to be true to clients, prospective clients or sponsors about the potential value of the coaching process or of me as a coach.
18. Carefully explain and strive to ensure that, prior to or at the initial meeting, my coaching client and sponsor(s) understand the nature of coaching, the nature and limits of confidentiality, financial arrangements, and any other terms of the coaching agreement.
19. Have a clear coaching service agreement with my clients and sponsor(s) before beginning the coaching relationship and honor this agreement. The agreement shall include the roles, responsibilities and rights of all parties involved.
20. Hold responsibility for being aware of and setting clear, appropriate and culturally sensitive boundaries that govern interactions, physical or otherwise, I may have with my clients or sponsor(s).
21. Avoid any sexual or romantic relationship with current clients or sponsor(s) or students, mentees or supervisees. Further, I will be alert to the possibility of any potential

sexual intimacy among the parties including my support staff and/or assistants and will take the appropriate action to address the issue or cancel the engagement in order to provide a safe environment overall.

22. Respect the client's right to terminate the coaching relationship at any point during the process, subject to the provisions of the agreement. I shall remain alert to indications that there is a shift in the value received from the coaching relationship.

23. Encourage the client or sponsor to make a change if I believe the client or sponsor would be better served by another coach or by another resource and suggest my client seek the services of other professionals when deemed necessary or appropriate.

Section 4: Confidentiality/Privacy

As a coach, I:

24. Maintain the strictest levels of confidentiality with all client and sponsor information unless release is required by law.

25. Have a clear agreement about how coaching information will be exchanged among coach, client and sponsor.

26. Have a clear agreement when acting as a coach, coach mentor, coaching supervisor or trainer, with both client and sponsor, student, mentee, or supervisee about the conditions under which confidentiality may not be maintained (e.g., illegal activity, pursuant to valid court order or subpoena; imminent or likely risk of danger to self or to others; etc) and make sure both client and sponsor, student, mentee, or supervisee voluntarily and knowingly agree in writing to that limit of confidentiality. Where I reasonably believe

that because one of the above circumstances is applicable, I may need to inform appropriate authorities.

27. Require all those who work with me in support of my clients to adhere to the ICF Code of Ethics, Number 26, Section 4, Confidentiality and Privacy Standards, and any other sections of the Code of Ethics that might be applicable.

Section 5: Continuing Development

As a coach, I:

28. Commit to the need for continued and ongoing development of my professional skills.

PART THREE: THE ICF PLEDGE OF ETHICS

As an ICF coach, I acknowledge and agree to honor my ethical and legal obligations to my coaching clients and sponsors, colleagues, and to the public at large. I pledge to comply with the ICF Code of Ethics and to practice these standards with those whom I coach, teach, mentor or supervise.

If I breach this Pledge of Ethics or any part of the ICF Code of Ethics, I agree that the ICF in its sole discretion may hold me accountable for so doing. I further agree that my accountability to the ICF for any breach may include sanctions, such as loss of my ICF Membership and/or my ICF Credentials.

For more information on the Ethical Conduct Review Process including links to file a complaint, contact ICF.

Adopted by the ICF Global Board of Directors June 2015.

Coaching Session Transcripts

CASE ONE COACHING SESSION TRANSCRIPT

Client:	Okay.
Coach:	We are recording now, great.
Client:	Wonderful, thank you.
Coach:	Okay, good. S., thanks for sharing with me a little bit about your business and your love of coaching, and your journey to this advanced designate and your time since Georgetown. You said you have an issue today you'd like to be coached on? Describe to me what you have on your mind.

Client: [00:01:00]	Okay. I'm in shared office space. Actually, I sub-lease space from friends who have a large real estate appraisal company. We have a lot of synergies in our shared business, shared clients. Recently I invited another friend of ours, who has a significant business... a friend of mine who has a significant business, also in real estate, to come and take some empty space in our shared office space. Now she has a very... she has thirteen people working for her, a very successful real estate business. She's one of my closest friends.
[00:02:00]	Over the years, I have helped her on a pro bono basis with her business, helping her hire people, helping her institute benefits. I really have served as a human resources person for her. I've never... One time I brought in an external consultant to help do her work, and then I charged her, but in all the years I've never charged her. I'm beginning to really resent it, because it's taking more and more of my time and because she's located in my premises here, she's located five doors down, the requests are much more often and much more significant. I'm now involved in all the hiring, and it's really taking up a significant piece of my time. I need to charge her, and I just can't feel comfortable doing it. I feel guilty, and in the meantime she runs a multimillion-dollar business, and I just... I'm really frustrated about it. I'm not moving forward.
Coach:	Yeah. Okay. It's the issue of... I'll play it back and make sure I've got it right. This is a colleague that you've had for a long time. She's now in your building, and you've done a lot of work for her pro bono, it's getting more and more, and it's taking more of your time. She runs a big business, and yet... You haven't charged her, and you're resentful. You kind of want to charge her, but something's holding you back.

Client:	That's right.
Coach:	Is that it?
[00:03:00] Client:	That's right, thank you. You've got it. I'm kind of waiting for her to offer, for her to say, "S. I really should be paying you for this," and I'm not moving forward to make the suggestion myself, like, "It's time."
Coach:	Yeah. Okay. If we coach, let's say, for about twenty minutes or thirty minutes or so, what would you like to walk away with at the end of our session? What would be helpful?
Client:	I would like to walk away with a resolution of how I handle this, and specific steps that I need to take, both to handle this particular situation and also on an ongoing basis, how to handle this on an ongoing basis. How to resolve this one, and to put something in place for the future.
[00:04:00] Coach:	The ones that might come up again, yeah. Okay, good. What is most important to you about this issue?
Client:	Not to be taken for granted. Being paid for my time is also important, but not to be taken for granted is probably at the core.
Coach:	That's how you're feeling now?
Client:	Yes.
Coach:	Tell me at what point in this relationship it went from, "I'll do her a favor," to being taken for granted.

Client: [00:05:00]	I think as she becomes more and more successful she is looking to me now as a way to save money. She should probably have either me as a... on an ongoing basis as a human resources person. She has twenty people working for her, thirteen here, and all around the country. The questions are becoming more complex, there are more issues. Either... When you're that size you need either to outsource it and hire an outside consultant to do the hiring-level human resources, or if it's me. As it's gotten bigger and more complicated, I realized that I've been feeling more and more taken for granted and even abused.
	I realized that it's a lot my fault because I haven't said, "Here, we need to draw the line now. It's too big, it's too complicated. It's too [crosstalk 00:05:42]."
Coach:	Yeah. You're acknowledging it's a lot your fault, yet you're waiting for her to make an offer?
Client:	That's right.
Coach:	Yeah.
Client:	That's exactly right.
Coach:	Yeah. Does this sound like anything else that goes on in your life, or is it just this one situation?
[00:06:00] Client:	That's a nice question. There are probably other times in my life that I let myself volunteer for too much and not draw the boundaries until I get upset about it. I allow it to happen to me, and I don't draw the boundaries, so then I get angry about it.
Coach:	When you get angry about it, what happens?
Client:	I get frustrated and stressed and internalize it, and maybe eventually I talk about it, but it usually takes a long time for me to push back.

Coach: [00:07:00]	When you say you talk about it, you mean when you get angry enough you confront the situation then, and you draw some boundaries?
Client:	Yeah. I think that I've matured to the point that I do that more, but it often takes a long time. I have, on my bulletin board in front of me, this little note that I had put as a mantra two years ago for what I was going to focus on two years ago, which is, "Calibrate commitment and satisfaction." Really try to figure out what I want to commit myself to and make sure that it's equal to the amount of satisfaction I get out of it.
Coach:	Nice.
Client: [00:08:00]	If they're out of sync, out of balance, then I realize I have to catch myself. It's something I talk to myself about, so this is a little bit like that, the commitment and satisfaction, so here I have this high level of commitment where I'll throw myself into things, and then I think about, "What kind of satisfaction am I getting?" It could be… Satisfaction could be emotional satisfaction, spiritual satisfaction, financial satisfaction, but it has to be balanced. It's something I'm aware that I have to be conscious of, or else I could throw myself into things that don't bring me any of those types of satisfaction. This is starting to be that.
Coach:	Yeah. I love that you have that there, and that's one of the ways you calibrate what you do. That thing you have on your wall came as a result of a situation like this, or this situation, or… ?
Client: [00:09:00]	Not this particular situation, but a taking stock at the end of the year, sort of evaluating where I am, "Where am I? Where do I want to focus my efforts moving forward? What are the things I know I need to be aware of?"
Coach:	Right.

Client:	I didn't think before this conversation that this situation also falls into one of these. If I was getting paid for it, then I would feel like that would be more in balance, but doing it just for the kindness and goodness of a person who is making millions of dollars is ridiculous.
Coach:	Yeah, and you kind of helped her get to that place, I would guess.
Client: [00:10:00]	Oh yeah. This also happens to be a person who I have mentored. She was an immigrant, and I hired her when I was human resources director. She knows. She will often talk about how she owes her entire career to me. She's practically a family member, and I brought her into... My offices are beautiful, and she was in a suburban, very modest location. This was a quantum leap for her to move down here.
Coach:	Wow. Yeah, so it really feels unequal now.
Client:	Right.
Coach:	What's at risk for you if you draw a boundary in this situation?
Client:	Well, she might be annoyed. She might put a value on the things that I do that might upset me. She might say, "Okay, I'll give you five hundred dollars." That would not be... Doing it for free is better than being underpaid for it, I think.
[00:11:00] Coach:	Yeah, so you want to be valued. You want to be valued for the work you do, and value has something to do with finance at this point, which... For sure.
Client:	Absolutely it does.
Coach:	Yeah. What's at risk is she might be annoyed; she might underpay you, right? She might offer something ...

Client:	The third thing is that if... I really am reluctant to come up with a monthly retainer, which would be, I think, a normal... A good solution in another situation. I'm afraid she would take advantage of that.
Coach:	In other words... Let me understand. If you were to make an offer of a retainer of a certain amount per month, she'd give you more... It's sort of like, again, being undervalued, right? She'd give you more work than that retainer would normally cover.
Client:	Absolutely. [Inaudible 00:11:54]
Coach:	Okay. What do you want?
[00:12:00] Client:	I've thought about this, and I'd like to just be able to give her the hours that I've worked and have her pay me for the hours that I've worked, to keep a log. I actually, this month, did keep a log of the hours that I worked. I think it's around fifteen hours, which is not... It's not a lot, but for free it's a lot.
Coach:	Yeah. Okay, so you thought about... You've taken some practical steps toward a log, knowing how many hours, thinking about asking to get paid for that, yet something's still holding you back. What do you think that is?
Client:	Well, this idea of being... Of her being annoyed about it. "I thought we're friends," kind of thing.
Coach:	What's at risk for you if she's annoyed?
Client:	Not much.
[00:13:00] Coach:	Okay.

Client:	Truly, not much. As I said, and the other piece is looking at it and say, "No, that's not worth a few thousand dollars," or, "That's not worth …" whatever I've put on it.
Coach:	Okay. If that were to happen, if she were to say, "No." Hire somebody else or thank you, or… What would… ?
Client:	That would really be fine.
Coach: [00:14:00]	Okay. That side of it is actually fine with you. You have in mind what you want, right? In terms of being some amount. It doesn't matter to me what amount, but you have an amount that would satisfy you for those fifteen hours. That's this month; next month it might be who knows what. You have an amount. You've thought it through in terms of what that amount is, you know the practical steps. What will it take from you to make a move?
Client:	I think just the resolution that I will do it. I think… She's leaving on vacation today or tomorrow, and it's the end of the month, so it seems like this is a good time to do it. A good time today before she leaves to talk to her about it and tell her that I'd like to give her this month, because I've spent a lot of hours on her work. I could see she's lacking it. She's delegating things to me.
Coach:	Even worse, huh?

Client: [00:15:00] [00:16:00]	Much worse. I'll talk to her about it. Up until now I've done... I've coached a few of her people. That's the other thing. Some things I... She has had a lot of turnover, so she really, really needs... She really needs my help. She could really use my help is the point, and I've coached a few of her people and it's made a really big difference in the way they come across to clients. I guess that's... The coaching is one thing. I love to do that, and it's good for me too. The coaching is good for me too, because any coaching I could do, I want to do, I want to take advantage of, especially if it's somebody who's really coachable. That has been an exciting piece for me. A couple of young people. Like I said, that's been really fun, but then I've been doing all this recruiting for her, which is like... I'd do it if I'm getting paid, but it's just annoying to... It's not even recruiting senior executives, it's these annoying people.
	It's stuff that I could do with my eyes closed, to tell you the truth. I've done it all the time. That's the stuff that I've been doing a lot of this month, because she's had a lot of turnover and she's needing a lot of new people, and I've run these ads for her and I've done all that. If I can, today before she leaves, talk to her about it, it will make me feel better, and just come up with a plan going forward. The coaching is probably one thing, and the recruiting is probably another.
Coach:	Yeah, I was going to ask you about that. Is there an offer in there somehow?
Client:	Yeah.
Coach:	Yeah? That there's... Well, is there an offer?

Client: [00:17:00]	Yeah. Maybe the offer to her is that we could split these two pieces apart and look at the coaching in one way, because that... They both really are important to her, and I coach her a lot too. Again, it's very hard to think about... How do I put a value on the different pieces of what I do for her?
Coach:	Yeah. If I could just kind of break this apart a minute, I saw your face when you said, "I coach her a lot too," and there seemed to be something about that that didn't... I don't know. It wasn't the same as when you said you loved the coaching and you coach her staff. There's something in there.
Client: [00:18:00]	Well, I do for her... I've had a mentoring relationship with her for twenty years, and as I said, I've been integral to her strategy in the business and it's been very... I've done consulting to her and I've done coaching with her, and since the program I've done a lot of coaching with her. I know it really has made a huge difference, and it is satisfying, although it's hard because she's not an easy person at all. She's very set in her ways, and I'm probably the only person who can ask her those challenging questions to think about. It's also very satisfying, because I look at her business and I know, and she knows too. That's why all this is so complicated, because we're ...
[00:19:00]	The thing is that now she's down here with me, and I need to set... She's been here since last summer. She moved in in August, but I do need to set it up going forward so that I can feel comfortable with that, and she can also feel comfortable. This is important.
Coach:	Is there a loss in there at all for you if you present her with some kind of proposal?

Client:	Yeah, I don't know. It would be sad if… I would be sad to give that up altogether, to give up the relationship, which I don't think is really necessary. Yeah, I do get personal satisfaction out of the coaching that I do with her and with her team. I really do, and I wouldn't mind doing some of these HR things, as I said, as long as I got paid.
Coach: [00:20:00]	Yeah. I'm kind of hearing, if I can play back this to you. I'm kind of hearing three buckets, and I don't know, tell me if that's what you mean, because maybe those offers are different for different buckets. One bucket is HR work, right? That bucket, it sounds like you don't have any ambivalence at all about counting up the number of hours and asking for a reasonable amount of pay. Would that be right?
Client:	Yes, that's correct.
Coach:	Okay. The second bucket is coaching her staff, which has made a great difference, you love it, and it gives you a lot of satisfaction. Is there a monetary value on that too, on that bucket too?
Client:	Yes.
Coach:	Okay, so you would make the same kind of proposal for that work?
Client:	Yeah.
Coach:	Okay. Then the third bucket, which is sort of like the second bucket, but different in a way, is the coaching you do with her herself. You've said you may be kind of the only one who can ask hard questions, and she has a lot of trust there, and all that. What about that bucket? Is that …

[00:21:00] **Client:**	I don't know that I could charge her for that. I don't know. It is by far the most valuable of the things I do for her, by far, but how could I put a monetary value? I don't know.
Coach:	Well, I don't know. I guess the question is, would you want to if you found a way, or is that something you feel like it's satisfying enough for you to see the growth of her business, and you have a piece in that, or will that continue to make you resentful?
Client:	I'm a little bit ambivalent about it, but I would do that for her. I would do that. If I could be paid for the other things... I sort of think at some point maybe she would know that she should pay me for that, but I can't.
Coach:	Well, that's what you thought about the other stuff, and that hasn't happened.
[00:22:00] **Client:**	You're right. You're right.
Coach:	That hasn't happened. Again, I don't know, are those the three buckets, or is there something else?
Client:	No, [inaudible 00:22:10] three things. I think coaching her, which is the most valuable and hard to put a price on it. I don't know what I would do with that. Coaching her staff, which is... We have regular every-other-week sessions, have real, formal coaching sessions right here in my office. I think it's great, and I think that she gets real financial value out of that. It saved her a client. Then the general HR jazz, which makes her life easier, and is critical in [inaudible 00:22:54] little place. Yeah, those are the three buckets.

[00:23:00]	
Coach:	Okay. What I heard from you clearly, and your facial expressions, is that the first two you have no problem putting a value on, asking for it is another thing. We'll get to that in a second. You have no problem putting a value on that. The third one... I don't know, I heard a little ambivalence there in terms of, "How would I ever value it?" Well, if she was anyone else how would you value it?
Client:	If she was an outside company that's easy. You'd just charge her the most for that.
Coach:	What keeps you from doing that? Just exploring.
Client: [00:24:00]	She's a very dear friend, and I've... First, she's a very dear friend. Two, I've been doing this for twenty years with her, and... now, since I went to Georgetown I started charging other people for that. I realized I'd always been giving that away, not just to her, but to everybody.
Coach:	Yeah, that's what makes you a good coach.
Client:	Would I change that? There's something that you do for friends. It just so happens that this friend built a huge business incorporating it.
Coach:	Okay, so let's just check in for a minute, because at the beginning you said you wanted to talk about this, you wanted to come to a resolution with some strategies of how to handle it. Where are you now with those strategies? Let's just check in.

[00:25:00] **Client:**	I think I've resolved that I need to handle this today for the present, this piece, which is I've been keeping some hours over this month, and this would be a good time to address… to have a conversation with her about it, to let her know that I have been tracking my hours this month, and that I'd like her to think about that and I'd like to come to an understanding with her of being compensated in some way for it. It doesn't have to be resolved today of what that is, but the fact that I want us to resolve it and to figure that out. We don't have to figure out how much or what, but that I want to resolve it and I'd like to be paid for the hours.
Coach:	Okay. How'd that feel when you said it out loud?
[00:26:00] **Client:**	A little bit excited about… Not excited about having the conversation, but it feels right. Feels like the right thing.
Coach:	Okay. I know you're probably not going to be excited about having the conversation, okay? I get that. You've had a long-term relationship with her. Now this, in some way, is going to change that relationship, right? It definitely will. I get that you're not excited. What is it… Is there anything else you have to resolve in yourself before you go into that conversation?

Client: [00:27:00]	I think I need to be comfortable that I am adding value, and I'm asking for something that has value. I think it's a personal self-respect that if I have a level of self-respect... It's not that she can't afford this. It's not that I'm asking for something that's not reasonable, or that she doesn't have to get from somewhere. I just have to do it, and if she's annoyed, so what? She's annoyed often at things I bring up to her and challenge her, but she does... The kind of person, when you're coaching someone and you hurt a nerve or something, it may not be comfortable, but you have to be okay in being in that. I know that she has enough respect for me that I think we can get through this.
Coach: [00:28:00]	Okay. Not comfortable, you know it's something that's bothered you for quite some time now, and you want to get rid of that resentment and that bother. Is there any role in making this request for separating out what you'd charge for and what you wouldn't?
	I think we've frozen here.
	Now you're back.
Client:	I had... This is my cell phone, so phone ...
Coach:	Yeah.
Client:	I'm sorry, I missed that.
Coach:	No, that's okay. I wondered if, in making a request... That's really what you're doing, even though you're not nailing down all the specifics today, you are making a request. In making that request, is there any role in specifying what you'd charge for and what you'd continue to do as a friend, as a coach?

[00:29:00] **Client:** [00:30:00]	That's a good idea. In fact, when I calculated the hours, I didn't calculate the hours that I spent with her, which are many. How do you break out those hours? Do you break them out by me sitting in her office or her coming to me, or us having a drink together, or… ? The hours that I've tracked are hours that I've spent either in bucket two or three, doing interviews for her and phone screens and going through resumes, got that bucket. Scheduling interviews, which I hate. The things… Interviews are okay, and I don't mind doing those, but the scheduling… That's one of the things I hate doing for myself. I'll outsource that, but I did it. The other thing is the coaching of her people. I think you've really helped me get some clarity around that.
Coach:	Okay.
Client:	Breaking out the ask.
Coach:	Okay. What… You said you want to talk to her today before she goes on vacation. Does that still feel like what you want to do?
Client:	Yeah. I think bringing it up. I don't think that… I think mentioning it to her. I think the conversation will probably not happen all in one chunk, but she is a good friend, and just mentioning to her, "There's been a lot of hours, and I'd like to talk to you about figuring out how I can get paid for these hours."
Coach:	Good.
Client: [00:31:00]	"We can talk about it in detail when you get back, but I just want you to know that I've been thinking about it."
Coach:	Yeah. That's a big step for you.
Client:	Yes.

Coach:	I'm wondering what will make sure... What will help you make sure that ball doesn't drop? Because it might be uncomfortable when she gets back.
Client:	I think if I put it in my calendar for when she gets back, I am pretty good about not... If something is in there that I need to do, I usually do it. I have it marked for myself, I think that will work.
Coach:	All right, good. I don't doubt your calendar. I'm questioning your resolve.
[00:32:00] Client:	Well, I think [crosstalk 00:31:52]. I think if something is in my calendar, I'll be uncomfortable enough with not ticking it off that it'll make me do it.
Coach:	All right, good. Okay. Great. As we finish up then, is there anything else about this, S., that will help you get to the resolution that you want?
Client:	I think really making sure that I do have that full conversation with her when she returns. Dropping it now as something I want to talk about, and then really making sure that I circle back to close the loop on that, so that I don't leave it as just this hanging [inaudible 00:32:44].
Coach:	Right, because that'll just create more resentment for you.
Client: [00:33:00]	Exactly, and as I said, as an ongoing basis... The idea of just addressing it with this list of hours, that's one thing, but be able to say, "Going forward, at the end of every month I'll give you a... send you a list of the hours so that you can pay me. If you decide that you don't want to do it, that's great, but I don't want to keep doing it for free."
Coach:	Right. I can see that all over your face, so... I wonder about the time she's on vacation, how you might use that to firm up your request or your offer.

Client: [00:34:00]	I don't think it needs to be all kinds of formal; just a short email would be good enough. There is some precedent, because as I said, last year, maybe two years ago, she had asked me to redo all of her HR materials, [crosstalk 00:34:04]. There was one time, and I purposely brought in an outside... another person to help me do it, because I knew that I would never be able to charge her for all... I would never be able to bring myself to charge her, but to charge somebody else's hours, that was much easier. At that point, I charged her for a few of my hours too, like three thousand dollars of my time, and it was something like five thousand of somebody else's time. It was a whole ...
	Even that in itself was very cheap for a whole handbook and all the procedures, the whole sweep of HR materials that she needed for her growing company. Offer letters, I mean, I put together the whole thing.
Coach:	Wow, that's a gift.
[00:35:00] Client:	A total gift, and for almost nothing, for... I think seven thousand dollars she had benefits programs. It was almost... The least she could've possibly gotten away with. Like I said, that was the only other time.
Coach:	There's some precedent for charging her, and no one died from it.
Client:	Yes, exactly. No one died from it.
Coach:	No one died from it.
Client:	Exactly.
Coach:	Good. That's kind of what I was thinking about is that... Back to your concern that she might offer you something too little, because clearly you got too little for that.

Client:	Yes.
Coach: [00:36:00]	That's what I'm wondering if you might give some thought to what that request is of her that's reasonable for you, and that actually she is getting something in return, which is the coaching you do for her. Anyway, that's what I'm wondering if... Not only putting it on your calendar, but in what way you might have to prepare for that subsequent conversation.
Client:	Yeah, it's great. Good.
Coach:	Okay. Anything else that we should talk about for this situation? I know it'll be hard, but I'll be rooting here for you.
Client:	Thank you. No, I think you've helped me clarify what I need to do, and I have some specific action that I need to take today, and also to follow up and to close the loop when she comes back. I feel like I have the... I've gained some clarity in what I need to do and my resolve to move forward.
Coach: [00:37:00]	Okay. Yeah, you seem... When you say it now, you seem more confident than you did before. I don't know if you are, but you seem... Yeah, you seem that way.
Client:	Yes.
Coach:	Good, okay. Now we ...
Client:	Thank you so much.
Coach:	You're welcome. Will you let me know the resolution?
Client:	I will.
Coach:	Okay. Either next time we talk or ...
Client:	Yes, absolutely.

Coach:	Good. Okay, very good. Well, we used most of our time here today, S. I hope that was okay. What learnings did you have from the session?
Client:	Yeah, I... Let's talk about a few learnings from this.
Coach:	Yeah, let's do that, that would be [crosstalk 00:37:27].
Client: [00:38:00]	I noticed that during the conversation... First of all, I felt very... You created a really great space for me, that you made me feel very comfortable in the conversation, and I felt that I was being heard. You restated a few times, and when it wasn't exactly, you were fine with letting go what you had originally thought and regrouped around my restatement of your... I noticed that. I noticed you checked in with me in the middle, which was really great, and I... I don't do that with my clients, like, "Is this what you're hoping to get?" I forgot exactly how you said it, but when you did it I noticed right away that you did it, and it was like two-thirds of the way in, which was really great. I learned something from that.
[00:39:00]	You commented on my... How I appeared and how I looked when I was talking, the somatics of it. Again, looking for what else was behind it. You started... If this brings up something else for me, and I think saw that it didn't seem to be going down that way, so you were trying different things, which I really appreciate, and I like that. I realized that you can't always zoom right into exactly the right thing, that you've got to play around a little bit to say, "Where is this going, and what's going to resonate?" I noticed that. I kept thinking, "I wish I could take notes," but you can't take notes in the middle of this.
Coach:	Yeah, but I'll send you the recording.
Client:	Yes. Oh, that's right, you recorded it. That's great. Thank you, good, I want to look at that again.

Coach:	Yeah.
Client:	Okay, well I'll have the recording, so that'll be great.
Coach:	Yeah, you'll be able to have that. I think it will be maybe useful both for you to hear it again when you're not in it, and also to notice what you're noticing right now, both from the situation point of view and from the coaching point of view. Is there something you wished would've happened that didn't? An area I could've explored but I didn't?
[00:40:00] Client:	I don't think so. You got to some things that made me uncomfortable, which is good, you know? I think that growth comes from some of those uncomfortable moments. I know you went there a little bit, and I know I know when that happens with my clients. I sort of... "Something is happening here." I have to tell myself, "Go with that, that's okay." I don't want to make people terribly uncomfortable, but sometimes that's where growth comes, I think.
Coach:	Yeah.
Client:	I don't know, I don't think so. I'm looking forward to watching it again.
Coach:	Yeah. That way you can... You'll be an observer then... You'll be in the balcony that time instead of in the dance floor.
Client:	Yes.
Coach:	Good. Okay.
[00:41:00] Client:	Okay, well P, thank you.
Coach:	Oh, you're welcome. You're welcome.

Client:	I think we're [inaudible 00:41:02]. Is there anything else that I should know, or… ?
Coach:	No, I'm really hoping you can have this conversation. I know you will. You're resolving to do it today, so I'm hoping you can do that, and I'm looking forward to hearing about it. My hope, of course, is that she says, "Oh my goodness, of course." That would be great, but …
Client:	She may.
Coach:	She may, who knows. Good. What I'll do, I'll send you the recording, and we probably should put another date on our calendar.
Client:	Yes, let's do that.
Coach:	Actually I'm going to stop this recording.

CASE ONE COACHING COMPETENCY BEHAVIORAL MARKERS WITH EVIDENCE

Competency 2: Creating the Coaching Agreement

COACHING COMPETENCY BEHAVIORAL MARKER	EVIDENCE OF MARKER
1. **Coach helps the client identify, or reconfirm, what s/he wants to accomplish in the session.** • Confirms and articulates back the agreement or focus for the session. • Asks the client to define desired outcome for the session.	2:00 There is an issue you want to be coached on? Describe what you have on your mind. 2:00 I'll play it back and make sure I've got it right. 24:00 Okay, so let's just check in for a minute, because at the beginning you said you wanted to talk about this, you wanted to come to a resolution with some strategies of how to handle it. Where are you now with those strategies? Let's just check in.
2. **Coach helps the client to define or reconfirm measures of success for what s/he wants to accomplish in the session.** • Asks what the evidence of success would. • Reflects back to the client the success measure(s) for the session.	3:00 What would you like to walk away with at the end of our session?

COACHING COMPETENCY BEHAVIORAL MARKER	EVIDENCE OF MARKER
3. Coach explores what is important or meaningful to the client about what s/he wants to accomplish in the session. • Inquires about the personal and/or professional relevance and/or significance of the client's topic. • Uses questions to help the client clarify what achieving the outcome would mean.	4:00 What is most important to you about this issue?
4. Coach helps the client define what the client believes they need to address or resolve in order to achieve what s/he wants to accomplish in the session. • Inquires about what issues would allow complete achievement of the goal. • Reflects heard issues back to the client. • Explores what must be resolved for the goal to be achieved.	24:00 Okay, so let's just check in for a minute, because at the beginning you said you wanted to talk about this, you wanted to come to a resolution with some strategies of how to handle it. Where are you now with those strategies? Let's just check in. 26:00 Is there anything else you have to resolve in yourself before you go into that conversation? 32:00 As we finish up then, is there anything else about this that will help you get to the resolution that you want? 39:00 Is there something you wished would've happened that didn't? An area I could've explored but I didn't?

COACHING COMPETENCY BEHAVIORAL MARKER	EVIDENCE OF MARKER
5. Coach continues conversation in direction of client's desired outcome unless the client indicates otherwise. • Recognizes emergence of new and/or competing session goal and recontracts as needed, as desired by client, the coaching session agreement and success measures.	*There were no new or competing goals identified and no recontracting was necessary. As seen in the transcript, the coach continued the conversation in the direction of the client's outcome.*

Competency 3: Creating Trust and Intimacy

COACHING COMPETENCY BEHAVIORAL MARKER	EVIDENCE OF MARKER
1. Coach acknowledges and respects the client's work in the coaching process. • Relates to the client through eye contact (for in-person or on-camera coaching); adapts to or matches the client's vocal rhythms; tracks with the client's language (body language or verbal language). • Understands, recognizes, and respects the client's self-concept/identity (the who). • Recognizes and affirms the client's courage and/or willingness to change.	8:00 I love that you have that there, and that's one of the ways you calibrate what you do.

COACHING COMPETENCY BEHAVIORAL MARKER	EVIDENCE OF MARKER
2. **Coach expresses support for the client.** • (*Support* is not the same as *caretaking*.) • Makes empathic comments. • Expresses confidence in the client's capabilities. • Reflects the client's progress. • Acknowledges successes, strengths, and unique characteristics.	7:00 Nice. 8:00 I love that you have that there, and that's one of the ways you calibrate what you do. 24:00 That's what makes you a good coach. 31:00 Yeah. That's a big step for you. 36:00 I know it'll be hard, but I'll be rooting here for you.
3. **Coach encourages and allows the client to fully express him/ herself.** • Uses silence that allows the client to process thinking and feeling. • Invites the client to disagree with the coach. • Affirmatively encourages the client to continue to express herself.	2:00 I'll play it back and make sure I got it right. 2:00 Is that it?

Competency 4: Coaching Presence

COACHING COMPETENCY BEHAVIORAL MARKER	EVIDENCE OF MARKER
1. Coach acts in response to both the whole person of the client and what the client wants to accomplish in the session. • "Whole person" includes, for example, when or how the client thinks, creates, and relates.	4:00 That's how you're feeling now? [*Indicates interest not only in the issue but also in the person.*] 5:00 Yeah. Does this sound like anything else that goes on in your life, or is it just this one situation? [*Coach is interested in the person beyond this specific challenge.*] 12:00 Yeah. Okay, so you thought about... You've taken some practical steps toward a log, knowing how many hours, thinking about asking to get paid for that, yet something's still holding you back. What do you think that is?

COACHING COMPETENCY BEHAVIORAL MARKER	EVIDENCE OF MARKER
2. **Coach is observant, empathetic and responsive.** • The coach treats the client's emotions respectfully, responsibly, and with unconditional positive regard.	8:00 I love that you have that there, and that's one of the ways you calibrate what you do. 10:00 Wow. Yeah, so it really feels unequal now. 11:00 Yeah, so you want to be valued. You want to be valued for the work you do, and value has something to do with finance at this point, which... For sure. 12:00 Let me understand. If you were to make an offer of a retainer of a certain amount per month, she'd give you more... It's sort of like, again, being undervalued, right? She'd give you more work than that retainer would normally cover.

COACHING COMPETENCY BEHAVIORAL MARKER	EVIDENCE OF MARKER
3. Coach notices and explores energy shifts in the client. • Shares observational feedback with the client when her vocal, verbal or body rhythms change.	17:00 Yeah. If I could just kind of break this apart a minute, I saw your face when you said, "I coach her a lot too," and there seemed to be something about that that didn't… I don't know. It wasn't the same as when you said you loved the coaching and you coach her staff. There's something in there. 23:00 Okay. What I heard from you clearly, and your facial expressions, is that the first two you have no problem putting a value on. The third one… I don't know, I heard a little ambivalence there in terms of, "How would I ever value it?"
4. Coach exhibits curiosity with the intent to learn more. • Genuinely and authentically inquires about the client's agenda. • Genuinely and authentically inquires about aspects of the client as a person.	10:00 What's at risk for you if you draw a boundary in this situation? 12:00 What's at risk for you if she's annoyed?

COACHING COMPETENCY BEHAVIORAL MARKER	EVIDENCE OF MARKER
5. Coach partners with the client by supporting the client to choose what happens in the session. • Extends an invitation to co-design or co-create session focus and direction. • Checks in on focus and direction during the session.	3:00 What would be helpful? 4:00 That's how you're feeling now? 11:00 OK, what do you want? 24:00 Let's check in for a minute.
6. Coach partners with the client by inviting the client to respond in any way to the coach's contributions and accepts the client's response. • Partners with the client by, if offering assessments or opinions, doing so as an invitation for the client to use or not use, as the client sees fit. • Hears and respects the client's frame of reference and thinking and, as appropriate, shares her own thinking and frame of reference without attachment.	5:00 You're acknowledging it's a lot your fault, yet you're waiting for her to make an offer? 11:00 So you want to be valued? 20:00 Yeah. I'm kind of hearing, if I can play back this to you. I'm kind of hearing three buckets, and I don't know, tell me if that's what you mean, because maybe those offers are different for different buckets. One bucket is HR work, right? That bucket, it sounds like you don't have any ambivalence at all about counting up the number of hours and asking for a reasonable amount of pay. Would that be right?

COACHING COMPETENCY BEHAVIORAL MARKER	EVIDENCE OF MARKER
7. Coach partners with the client by playing back the client's expressed possibilities for the client to choose from. • Recognizes and reflects when, where, and with whom the client is at choice. • Paraphrases or clarifies coach's understanding of choices by the client.	19:00 Yeah. I'm kind of hearing, if I can play back this to you. I'm kind of hearing three buckets. One bucket is HR work, right? Would that be right? 23:00 Okay. What I heard from you clearly, and your facial expressions, is that the first two you have no problem putting a value on. The third one… I don't know, I heard a little ambivalence there in terms of, "How would I ever value it?"
8. Coach partners with the client by encouraging the client to formulate his or her own learning. • Inquires about and/or champions the client's capability to assess his/her learning. • Inquires about the client's intuition and interpretation of the client's being, situation, and/or actions.	32:00 Is there anything else about this that will help you get to the resolution you want? 37:00 What learnings did you have from the session?

Competency 5: Active Listening

COACHING COMPETENCY BEHAVIORAL MARKER	EVIDENCE OF MARKER
1. Coach's questions and observations are customized by using what the coach has learned about whom the client is and the client's situation. • Listens to client processes, not only the specific meaning of client's language and concepts. • Uses what the client has said to form questions, not only about the situation but about the client's being.	2:00 Okay. It's the issue of... I'll play it back and make sure I've got it right. This is a colleague that you've had for a long time. She's now in your building, and you've done a lot of work for her pro bono, it's getting more and more, and it's taking more of your time. She runs a big business, and yet... You haven't charged her, and you're resentful. You kind of want to charge her, but something's holding you back. 4:00 Tell me at what point in this relationship it went from "I'll do her a favor," to being taken for granted. 10:00 Wow. Yeah, so it really feels unequal now. 11:00 Yeah, so you want to be valued. You want to be valued for the work you do, and value has something to do with finance at this point, which... For sure. 12:00 Yeah. Okay, so you thought about... You've taken some practical steps toward a log, knowing how many hours, thinking about asking to get paid for that, yet something's still holding you back. What do you think that is?

COACHING COMPETENCY BEHAVIORAL MARKER	EVIDENCE OF MARKER
(continued)	22:00 Okay. What I heard from you clearly, and your facial expressions, is that the first two you have no problem putting a value on, asking for it is another thing. We'll get to that in a second. You have no problem putting a value on that. The third one... I don't know, I heard a little ambivalence there in terms of, "How would I ever value it?" Well, if she was anyone else how would you value it?
2. Coach inquires about or explores thre client's use of language. • Uses or incorporates the client's actual words into coach's paraphrasing, summarizing or questioning.	5:00 You're acknowledging it's a lot your fault, yet you're waiting for her to make an offer? 6:00 When you say you talk about it, you mean when you get angry enough you confront the situation then, and you draw some conclusions? 11:00 What's at risk is she might be annoyed; she might underpay you, right? She might offer something ...

COACHING COMPETENCY BEHAVIORAL MARKER	EVIDENCE OF MARKER
3. Coach inquires about or explores the client's emotions. • Asks about or reflects the client's emotions by recognizing mood, tone, affect, images or values.	4:00 That's how you're feeling now? 6:00 When you get angry about it, what happens? 7:00 When you say you talk about it, you mean when you get angry enough you confront the situation then, and you draw some boundaries? 33:00 Right, I can see that all over your face.
4. Coach inquires about or explores the client's tone of voice, pace of speech or inflection as appropriate. • Shares observational feedback when the client's vocal intonation or verbal pacing changes.	22:00 Okay. What I heard from you clearly, and your facial expressions, is that the first two you have no problem putting a value on, asking for it is another thing. We'll get to that in a second. You have no problem putting a value on that. The third one... I don't know, I heard a little ambivalence there in terms of, "How would I ever value it?" Well, if she was anyone else how would you value it? 37:00 When you say it now, you seem more confident than you did before.
5. Coach inquires about or explores the client's behaviors • Shares observational feedback when the client's vocal intonation or verbal pacing changes.	35:00 Good. That's kind of what I was thinking about is that... Back to your concern that she might offer you something too little, because clearly you got too little for that.

COACHING COMPETENCY BEHAVIORAL MARKER	EVIDENCE OF MARKER
6. Coach inquires about or explores how the client perceives his/her world. • Asks about, identifies, or tests the client's beliefs, assumptions, values, and perspectives.	5:00 Does this sound like anything else that goes on in your life or is it just this one situation? 35:00 Good. That's kind of what I was thinking about is that… Back to your concern that she might offer you something too little, because clearly you got too little for that.
7. When appropriate, coach is quiet and gives client time to think. • When listening to a response, coach gives sufficient time for the client to answer.	6:00 *Prior to this question, the coach was quiet.* 7:00 *Prior to "nice," coach was quiet.* *There are many other examples where the coach gave the client time to answer. These are not always identifiable from the transcript.*

Competency 6: Powerful Questioning

COACHING COMPETENCY BEHAVIORAL MARKER	EVIDENCE OF MARKER
1. **Coach asks questions about the client; his/her way of thinking, assumptions, beliefs, values, needs, wants, etc.** • Inquires about thinking, assumptions, beliefs, and values without necessarily using those exact words in the coaching.	4:00 Tell me at what point in this relationship it went from, "I'll do her a favor," to being taken for granted. 19:00 Is there a loss in there at all for you if you present her with some kind of proposal? 21:00 Well, I don't know. I guess the question is, would you want to if you found a way, or is that something you feel like it's satisfying enough for you to see the growth of her business, and you have a piece in that, or will that continue to make you resentful? 25:00 Okay. How'd that feel when you said it out loud?

COACHING COMPETENCY BEHAVIORAL MARKER	EVIDENCE OF MARKER
2. Coach's questions help the client explore beyond his/her current thinking to new or expanded ways of thinking about himself/herself. • Questions and observations challenge the client's thinking. (Not in all sessions.) • Questions and observations move the client out of the current story she is telling and help her look forward.	5:00 Yeah. You're acknowledging it's a lot your fault, yet you're waiting for her to make an offer? 6:00 When you get angry about it, what happens? 7:00 When you say you talk about it, you mean when you get angry enough you confront the situation then, and you draw some boundaries? 10:00 What's at risk for you if you draw a boundary in this situation? 12:00 Yeah. Okay, so you thought about… You've taken some practical steps toward a log, knowing how many hours, thinking about asking to get paid for that, yet something's still holding you back. What do you think that is? 12:00 What's at risk for you if she's annoyed? 14:00 Okay. That side of it is actually fine with you. You have in mind what you want, right? In terms of being some amount. It doesn't matter to me what amount, but you have an amount that would satisfy you for those fifteen hours. That's this month, next month it might be who knows what. You have an amount. You've thought it through

COACHING COMPETENCY BEHAVIORAL MARKER	EVIDENCE OF MARKER
(continued)	in terms of what that amount is, you know the practical steps. What will it take from you to make a move?
	21:00 Well, I don't know. I guess the question is, would you want to if you found a way, or is that something you feel like it's satisfying enough for you to see the growth of her business, and you have a piece in that, or will that continue to make you resentful?
	22:00 Well, if she was anyone else how would you value it?
	23:00 What keeps you from doing that? Just exploring.

COACHING COMPETENCY BEHAVIORAL MARKER	EVIDENCE OF MARKER
3. Coach's questions help the client explore beyond his/her current thinking to new or expanded ways of thinking about his/her situation. • Asks the client to look at the situation from different perspectives. • Asks questions that help the client reframe a problem or challenge to a more empowering frame for the client.	5:00 Yeah. Does this sound like anything else that goes on in your life, or is it just this one situation? 16:00 Yeah, I was going to ask you about that. Is there an offer in there somehow? 28:00 In making that request, is there any role in specifying what you'd charge for and what you'd continue to do as a friend, as a coach? 30:00 Okay. What... You said you want to talk to her today before she goes on vacation. Does that still feel like what you want to do? 36:00 Anything else that we should talk about for this situation?
4. Coach's questions help the client explore beyond current thinking towards the outcome s/he desires. • Asks the client to imagine/picture/articulate her desired future. • Questions help the client create new scenarios that would create success for her goal.	12:00 Okay. What do you want? 14:00 What will it take from you to make a move? 19:00 Is there a loss in there at all for you if you present her with some kind of proposal?

COACHING COMPETENCY BEHAVIORAL MARKER	EVIDENCE OF MARKER
5. Coach asks clear, direct, primarily open-ended questions, one at a time, at a pace that allows for thinking and reflection by the client. • Asks questions that provoke inquiry—questions that cannot be answered literally with a yes or a no. • Allows the client to think before inserting another question.	14:00 What will it take from you to make a move? 25:00 Okay. How'd that feel when you said it out loud?
6. Coach's questions use the client's language and elements of the client's learning style and frame of reference. • Understands and works with the client's learning style (e.g., if client's preferred learning style is by doing, conceptualizing, experimenting, reflecting, visualizing, storytelling, etc.).	6:00 When you get angry about it what happens? 16:00 Is there an offer in there somehow?
7. Coach's questions are not leading, i.e. do not contain a conclusion or direction.	23:00 What keeps you from doing that? 30:00 Does that still feel like what you want to do?

Competency 7: Direct Communication

COACHING COMPETENCY BEHAVIORAL MARKER	EVIDENCE OF MARKER
1. Coach shares observations, intuitions, comments, thoughts and feelings to serve the client's learning or forward movement. • Coach's statements help the client explore beyond her current thinking to new or expanded ways of thinking. • Coach's statements help the client explore beyond current thinking towards the outcome she desires.	37:00 When you say it now, you seem more confident than you did before. I don't know if you are, but you seem that way.
2. Coach shares observations, intuitions, comments, thoughts and feelings without any attachment to them being right. • Shares beliefs and assessments, not held as truths. • When sharing observations, intuition, comments, thoughts or feelings, coach clearly communicates that they are an "offer" for the client to respond to in any way she chooses.	35:00 Good. That's kind of what I was thinking about is that… Back to your concern that she might offer you something too little, because clearly you got too little for that.

COACHING COMPETENCY BEHAVIORAL MARKER	EVIDENCE OF MARKER
3. Coach uses the client's language or language that reflects the client's way of speaking. • Uses the client's language as well as introducing new language. • Uses the client's words, speed, speech patterns, etc.	2:00 Yeah. Okay. It's the issue of… I'll play it back and make sure I've got it right. This is a colleague that you've had for a long time. She's now in your building, and you've done a lot of work for her pro bono, it's getting more and more, and it's taking more of your time. She runs a big business, and yet… You haven't charged her, and you're resentful. You kind of want to charge her, but something's holding you back. 28:00 That's really what you're doing, even though you're not nailing down all the specifics today. 10:00 Wow. Yeah, so it really feels unequal now. 11:00 Yeah, so you want to be valued. You want to be valued for the work you do, and value has something to do with finance at this point.
4. Coach's language is generally clear and concise. • When sharing observations, intuitions, comments, thoughts or feelings, coach clearly communicates and articulates in a manner that is easily and readily understood by the client.	8:00 I love that you have that there, and that's one of the ways you calibrate what you do. 9:00 You kind of helped her get to this place, I would guess.

COACHING COMPETENCY BEHAVIORAL MARKER	EVIDENCE OF MARKER
5. The coach allows the client to do most of the talking. • Talks considerably less than the client (in totality of conversation).	*The transcript shows that the client clearly speaks more. See 1:00, 5:00, 7:00, 8:00, 9:00, 12:00 14:00-16:00, 18:00, 27:00.*
6. Coach allows the client to complete speaking without interrupting unless there is a stated coaching purpose to do so. • If the coach does not interrupt the client during the session, mark the marker. • If the coach interrupts on one or two occasions with a stated coaching purpose, mark the marker. • If the coach interrupts without a stated coaching purpose or interrupts frequently, do not mark the marker.	*There were no interruptions noted.*

Competency 8: Creating Awareness

COACHING COMPETENCY BEHAVIORAL MARKER	EVIDENCE OF MARKER
• 1. Coach invites client to state and/or explore his/her learning in the session about her/his situation (the what). • Asks about insights, learnings, and take-aways during and/or at end of session	37:00 What learnings did you have from the session? 37:00 Will you let me know the resolution?
• 2. Coach invites client to state and/or explore his/her learning in the session about her/himself (the who). • Inquires how new awareness/learning influences the client's behavior or way of being in the situation or perceiving herself.	12:00 You've taken some practical steps toward a log, knowing how many hours, thinking about asking to get paid for that, yet something's still holding you back. What do you think that is? 37:00 What learnings did you have from the session?

COACHING COMPETENCY BEHAVIORAL MARKER	EVIDENCE OF MARKER
• 3. Coach shares what s/he is noticing about the client and/or the client's situation, and seeks the client's input or exploration. • As evidenced by coach inquiring about or noticing the client's emotions, body language, tone of voice, patterns of thought, and patterns of language.	10:00 Wow. Yeah, so it really feels unequal now. 12:00 Yeah. Okay, so you thought about... You've taken some practical steps toward a log, knowing how many hours, thinking about asking to get paid for that, yet something's still holding you back. What do you think that is? 13:00 Okay. If that were to happen, if she were to say, "No." Hire somebody else or thank you, or... What would... ? 16:00 Yeah, I was going to ask you about that. Is there an offer in there somehow? 20:00 Yeah. I'm kind of hearing, if I can play back this to you. I'm kind of hearing three buckets, and I don't know, tell me if that's what you mean, because maybe those offers are different for different buckets. One bucket is HR work, right? That bucket, it sounds like you don't have any ambivalence at all about counting up the number of hours and asking for a reasonable amount of pay. Would that be right? 22:00 That hasn't happened. Again, I don't know, are those the three buckets, or is there something else?

COACHING COMPETENCY BEHAVIORAL MARKER	EVIDENCE OF MARKER
• 4. Coach invites client to consider how s/he will use new learning from the coaching. • States or links the client's new learning to the client's session or meta-goal, as a result of the coaching session process. • Invites the client to broaden the impact of learning to other situations or ways of being.	5:00 Does this sound like anything else that goes on in your life or is it just this one situation? 13:00 If that were to happen, if she were to say "No, hire somebody else or thank you." What would your response be?
• 5. Coach's questions, intuitions and observations have the potential to create new learning for the client. • Coach asks permission to consult, teach or mentor occasionally when in service of the client's immediate or longer-term agenda. • Coach's sharing of her own ideas, options, intuition or wisdom has the potential to expand the client's awareness and choice points or advance the client's agenda.	9:00 You kind of helped her get to this place, I would guess. 11:00 So you want to be valued for the work you do, and value has something to do with finance at this point?

Competencies 9, 10, and 11: Designing Actions, Planning and Goal Setting, and Managing Progress and Accountability

COACHING COMPETENCY BEHAVIORAL MARKER	EVIDENCE OF MARKER
1. Coach invites or allows client to explore progress towards what s/he want to accomplish in the session. • Inquires about the client's progress toward the goal. • Follows up on the client's stated progress, or lack of progress, toward the goal.	24:00 Where are you now with those strategies? Let's just check in.
2. Coach assists the client to design what actions/thinking client will do after the session in order for the client to continue moving toward the client's desired outcomes. • Actions may look like: further thinking; additional feeling or living with an idea; self-inquiry; behavior change; task completion; research; or experimentation.	26:00 Is there anything else you have to resolve in yourself before you go into that conversation? 31:00 What will help you make sure that ball doesn't drop? 33:00 I wonder about the time she's on vacation, how you might use that to firm up your request or your offer. 36:00 in what way might you have to prepare for that subsequent conversation. 36:00 Anything else that we should talk about for this situation?

COACHING COMPETENCY BEHAVIORAL MARKER	EVIDENCE OF MARKER
3. Coach invites or allows client to consider her/his path forward, including, as appropriate, support mechanisms, resources and potential barriers. • Explores likelihood of an action to occur in the future (e.g. use of a scaling question). • Inquires about the client's feeling about the action. • Tests the client's level of willingness to execute.	31:00 I'm wondering what will make sure… What will help you make sure that ball doesn't drop? Because it might be uncomfortable when she gets back. 31:00 I don't doubt your calendar. I'm questioning your resolve. 36:00 Not only putting it on your calendar, but in what way you might have to prepare for that subsequent conversation.
4. Coach assists the client to design the best methods of accountability for her/himself. • Coach can serve as an accountability partner on occasion. • Inquires about other forms of support for client accountability structures.	32:00 is there anything else about this that will help you get to the resolution that you want? 37:00 Will you let me know the resolution?

COACHING COMPETENCY BEHAVIORAL MARKER	EVIDENCE OF MARKER
5. **Coach partners with the client to close the session.** • Invites the client to consider how she wants to complete the session. • Checks in with the client on what topics the client is complete with and what.	32:00 As we finish up then, is there anything else about this that will help you get to the resolution that you want? 36:00 Anything else that we should talk about for this situation? I know it'll be hard, but I'll be rooting here for you. 39:00 Is there something you wished would've happened that didn't? An area I could've explored but I didn't?
6. **Coach notices and reflects client's progress.** • Celebrates the client's success when the client executes on agreed action commitments. • Inquires about obstacles that got in the way of the client's efforts to follow through on actions.	8:00 I love that you have that there. 24:00 Yeah, that's what makes you a good coach. 31:00 That's a big step for you.

CASE TWO COACHING SESSION TRANSCRIPT

Coach:	I am starting the recording and I want to be sure that it's okay for me to record this session.
Client:	It's okay.

Coach:	Okay, great, because that has to be also in the recording if we're going to be doing that. So let's focus on what you want to accomplish today. By the end of the session, what would you like to see differently regarding your leadership?
[00:00:30] Client:	At the end of this session I would like to take more distance and really feel comfortable with myself as a chapter leader even if things, projects, tasks are not being accomplished in the time frame that is reasonable for me and feel okay with that.
[00:01:00] Coach:	How will you know that you feel okay with it?
Client: [00:01:30]	I think I will feel it. I will really feel it, I will feel comfortable with myself, I will just let it go and be relaxed with that. Taking into consideration the fact that I know that people around me will have the resources and the capabilities to do it ultimately.
Coach:	It seems that one of the talents is to remember that, is it?
Client:	Yes.

Coach:	So by the end of the session today because this is what you are going to accomplish in the future when you are with your team, but by the end of the session today, specifically, what will you want to accomplish around your leadership?
[00:02:00] Client: [00:02:30]	Really let it go. Let it go, let it go, and really be confident that people around me who applied to be board members of the organization are the good people so really trust them more and maybe trust myself more as well.
[00:03:00] Coach:	Trusting you is also related to what you said before about being more confident as a leader.
Client:	Yes.
Coach:	It is in the context within the last sessions of who you want to be as a leader.
Client:	Absolutely.
Coach:	What makes this important to you today? What makes building this confidence and trusting yourself, why is this important for you today?

[00:03:30] **Client:** [00:04:00] [00:04:30]	It is important really in my eyes because if I don't do that I don't feel okay. I don't feel well. So in order for me to feel better to really let things just happen, even if we're saying it is my duty and unless I'm really aware of it, it's my duty to be the process guarantee in a way and I see my role like that. If I do that, if I achieve that, I would really feel as the leader I want to be.
Coach:	Where would you like to start exploring all of the things you are bringing up here? Because you talk about confidence, you talk about trust; you talked about believing in your people. You talked about remembering that you have your own resources. Where will you think will be a good place?
[00:05:00] **Client:**	What would I think would be …
Coach:	A good place to start exploring.
Client:	A good place. Well, I think that the good place would be within myself. Inside of me.
Coach:	Okay, so inside of you, around what question would you like to answer or explore?

[00:05:30] **Client:** [00:06:00]	Yup, yeah, yeah, yeah, yeah. The question that I sometimes ask myself is the family one and why is it so important for you that people would have listed the same path as you have in order to achieve what you want to achieve? Because people might have different targets, different preferences, different points of view, opinions, whatsoever. The fact is that I'm pretty aware of it but this fact that sometimes I get a bit nervous or frustrated when it comes to moving forward.
[00:06:30] **Coach:**	What is your hypothesis of what is going on there? What do you think is coming, that need that people will think like you, do with you?
Client: [00:07:00]	The tendency, the envy, the desire to have something concrete which in a way is rather difficult because sometimes and especially in our profession making things happen in a very concrete way is not always easy. It's even really challenging.
Coach:	Even this conversation is not in concrete!

Client: [00:07:30] [00:08:00]	Absolutely, absolutely and sometimes, I'm just wondering now and you made me aware of it, I'm not even aware myself if what I would like to see very concretely, I'm really not even aware of what it is myself so that's maybe the dilemma. If I'm not aware myself of what I want to see and realize how could people be able to see that in a concrete way as I would like them to see?
Coach:	Now that you realize that, now that you have the realization, who would you like to be in this situation as a leader? You have to design yourself as a leader, who do you want to be as a leader?
[00:08:30] Client: [00:09:00]	If I take a metaphor because I'm just thinking about it, I would like, because I told you last time that for me a leader is among others someone who say, whom people are following. I wouldn't say blindly, but at least I would say whenever there is a tempest or nice weather someone people are following and if I think this metaphor I would say, in French we say [foreign language] You see in the middle of the ocean you have sometimes this tower with a light, I don't know how we say that in English but you see what I mean, just to guide the …
Coach:	The lighthouse, I think. Or [foreign language] in Spanish, yeah.

Client:	To guide the boats and so forth and yes, so that's what comes to my mind when you ask me the question.
[00:09:30] Coach:	So if you will be a lighthouse and you guide like in the middle for the boat how would that look like and how would you show up as a leader?
Client:	Well, be there whenever is necessary but not necessarily always be there.
[00:10:00] Coach:	Isn't the thing because in your voice different than before. You sound like more confident, you said "be there," like in the way that it came out, it came out like with a confidence you were talking about.
Client: [00:10:30] [00:11:00] [00:11:30]	Yes but when I just pronounced it the word "be there" it made think of the competence presence of the coach and in fact being present is so powerful and sometimes we can be present just by practice doing nothing but just be there. In fact I'm going to, I told you in introduction, to tell how I don't like, I don't remember if it's the last one or just the, not the last one, but the one before our meeting before the board. We were not all of us present but just to give you an example, we decided that every member would send for a deadline his dates in order to feed our internet site.

[00:12:00] [00:12:30] [00:13:00]	Some of them didn't do it. We are eight of us, maybe four people did it and progressively two others didn't and at that very moment I just reminded people that we had agreed that we would all challenge each other and that if we set a deadline that everybody would stick to this deadline and at a certain moment one new member whom I don't know much, I'm just getting to know people better, got upset not because of my words but at this very moment, one of the new members as well rather senior guy, around 60 years, just told, "Hey guys, that's just a fact. We decided that everybody would do it and it only takes, if we just take time, 15 minutes, not more, to do it. So it's not that complicated," and so forth and at a certain moment the lady nearly exploded and nearly, "Well if it's like that, I'm going to quit whatsoever," and I have to tell you that at that very moment, at a certain moment, I said "Why is he interfering, why is he saying that?" I wanted to say "Hey stop!" But I didn't do anything. I didn't do anything; I just listened and tried to question a position trying quickly to understand and realizing what was happening.

[00:13:30] [00:14:00] [00:14:30] [00:15:00]	Why did he interfere may be because of course the guy got upset himself but she hadn't done it. She got emotionally touched and maybe too much and said, "Hey you are attacking me, so if you are reacting that way then I will quit!" So what does it say about these two persons? I didn't say anything, I just listened and then at a certain moment, I have to even say that I was happy that this happened because it gave me the opportunity to see how people also could interact without that I'm involved in the conversation. I don't know if I had the right attitude but I just let them do, waited until the climate and the mood became a bit cooler and then the guy excused himself, said, "Okay I didn't want to attack you personally" and then yes and the lady calm downed down also, "Yeah, okay I may be a bit emotionally too expressive whatsoever" and finally things solved it by themselves without that I had to say a word. I was so happy.
Coach:	What do you think of this scene, if you put a little distance and you look at the scene like a helicopter perspective, and you see that, you were talking before, what does this say about them but what does this say about you?

[00:15:30] **Client:** [00:16:00]	Yes, absolutely! That's also a very important part. I think that it also says something new about me is say compared to last year I just watched. I didn't interfere, and I didn't want to interfere. Well I wanted unconsciously, maybe unconsciously, I just tried to shut up, you know? In a silent way. But there was a little voice inside of me saying "Hey you, don't say anything, just wait." Just wait because I also wanted …
Coach:	And that voice, sorry for interrupting you, but that voice was telling you to wait, where do you think it was coming from?
[00:16:30] **Client:**	That voice, my little voice. Well I think from my heart. From my heart and from my head I would say.
Coach:	Okay so how do you think that this what you're saying affects your leadership? What happened when this was coming from your heart different than from your head? How does this affect who you are as a leader?

[00:17:00] **Client:** [00:17:30]	Well, I think and I hope that it shows that I'm a leader who above others focuses on the human side on the relationship, on the quality of the relationships between people and that I'm not at all in an autocratic way, which some people at a certain moment previously told me that I was, you see? So I'm working on that.
Coach: [00:18:00]	I heard in this conversation a couple of times where you had some realizations. One when you talk about discovering who you really are as a leader before people have figured out who you are like you knowing yourself. The second one here about the learning about following your heart and from that the relationship and how that affects who you are a leader? How can you apply these learnings to the question that we have today around building confidence, developing trust in yourself, and being the leader you want to be?

[00:18:30] **Client:** [00:19:00] [00:19:30] [00:20:00]	I think that what I realized is that the more I don't put the focus on even the unconscious desire to be appreciated, the more comfortable I feel. In fact, when I say I think that being too autocratic, too interfering, was a way of protecting myself and also this desire to be appreciated, loved, and so forth because I know that I need that. I need that from people around me and not that from one moment to another I suddenly become more mature. I don't know what happened but there's a sort of click [claps] what happened, which happened, again this little voice telling me "Hey. Just let it go. You know who you are and you don't have to be, you don't have to try to be so much appreciated as you would desire because there's no need to." There's no need to. Also, I have in a way, maybe not totally, stopped asking myself the question do people appreciate me or not? I think that I asked myself this question previously, even unconsciously, and now less.
[00:20:30] **Coach:**	And when you are less concerned about that, what is the consequence?

Client: [00:21:00]	I think that the consequence is that people might do things, just go on with what they are busy with, without even that I'm aware of. What makes me think that people are not busy with what they are responsible for even if they don't tell me. Am I being understandable, yeah?
Coach: [00:21:30]	What you're saying is it's about trusting people, is that it? That you're trusting people even without seeing them.
Client:	Absolutely, absolutely. So just trust them that the projects will be finalized. If they are not, well we'll see at that moment but not just put the horses before the cart.
[00:22:00] Coach:	We need to start wrapping up. Based on our conversation and what you wanted to accomplish in this session, where are you?
Client: [00:22:30] [00:23:00]	Where am I? I'm certainly a bit ahead of where I was before I would say a couple of months ago and even considering our session, even a little bit further as compared to the beginning because that's true, well I mentioned and you mentioned just after me the word trust, I think that is something very important and I'm aware of it because you see for me, it's one of the foundations of the good working of the team. Without trust, it's really difficult to move on.

Coach: [00:23:30]	Going back to the metaphor that you used at the beginning of the lighthouse and when you talk about "be there" and what you're saying now about this trust, like trust and be there, trust in yourself in just being there, and knowing when to participate, not to participate, ready to trust in you, trust in your team. How do you think that can translate into steps or actions, something you can do after this session?
Client: [00:24:00]	I think that in a way I've already started, but I will go on. It's just that if I want to know something whatsoever but the two thing is just to go on, just ask them in a very open way, "Okay, where are you so far about that?" Just give them my trust that it will be okay and also if they need whatever, I'm there. That's one.

[00:24:30] [00:25:00] [00:25:30] [00:26:00]	Second, I also told you that I've already taken the decision to step down as a chapter leader next year in order to leave the place to [name]. So the second step is order yourself to give some space to [name] in order to take the lead on some project. You know even if I'm still there and I still like to, I still have this little desire to control even if I'm controlling myself but at least we'll say to let her some space. By the way, I asked Matt about this recording, you remember, about we say about who's doing you? And so forth and then he told me that he doesn't find it back but we will end with the session with Matt before I end the phone so it will be done very soon. So that's the second I've already taken and that I will continue to take even if I'm still there. I'm really still there and I also want to play my role as a mentor to [name] of course.

Coach: [00:26:30]	Just to make a comment, so when you're asking questions you said a couple of things that I wanted to bring to your attention. When you ask questions and when you're working with people and delegating activities you see you're going to be trusting them. So it seems that you may bring consciously your belief that they can be trusted and you are choosing to trust them. And at the same time you are going to support them so I want to be supportive I want to be able to think I will be there and at the same time be more comfortable in delegating tasks to other people [unintelligible]. Okay, how do you want to wrap up this session today?
[00:27:00] Client:	In a very nice way. The question is how.
Coach:	How is it in a nice way, in a very nice way, how is it?
Client: [00:27:30]	How in a nice way, let's do it in a nice way. In making myself, and you, but more myself the promise that I will keep on having this attitude and state of mind whatever happens.

Coach:	I am asking you also if you want to consider as a possibility how you can use this not only for your work as a volunteer but also in your personal life. How some conversations came up today about trust, confidence, control can be in some way showing up in other parts of your personal life that you cannot simply take advantage of.
[00:28:00] Client:	Absolutely, I agree. Finally, thank you very much!
Coach:	Thank you! Congratulations on your work. Is it okay for me to still, use this recording for people who are …
Client:	If you think that it might be useful to other people feel free, absolutely.
Coach:	Okay, great thank you, yeah. I think that will be the case so thank you for that and let's set up some time to meet, you want in a month from now? So we can follow up on today?

CASE TWO COACHING COMPETENCY BEHAVIORAL MARKERS WITH EVIDENCE

Competency 2: Creating the Coaching Agreement

COACHING COMPETENCY BEHAVIORAL MARKER	EVIDENCE OF MARKER
1. Coach helps the client identify, or reconfirm, what s/he wants to accomplish in the session. • Confirms and articulates back the agreement or focus for the session. • Asks the client to define the desired outcome for the session.	1:00 So let's focus on what you want to accomplish today. By the end of the session, what would you like to see differently regarding your leadership? 1:00 How will you know you feel OK with it?
2. Coach helps the client to define or confirm measures of success for what s/he wants to accomplish in the session. • Asks what the evidence of success would. • Reflects back to the client the success measure for the session.	1:30 How will you know that you feel okay with it? 1:30 So by the end of the session today because this is what you are going to accomplish in the future when you are with your team, but by the end of the session. Specifically, what will you want to accomplish around your leadership?

COACHING COMPETENCY BEHAVIORAL MARKER	EVIDENCE OF MARKER
3. Coach explores what is important or meaningful to the client about what s/he wants to accomplish in the session. • Inquires about the personal and/or professional relevance and/or significance of the client's topic. • Uses questions to help the client clarify what achieving the outcome would mean.	3:00 What makes this important to you today? What makes building this confidence and trusting yourself, why is this important for you today?
4. Coach helps the client define what the client believes they need to address or resolve in order to achieve what s/he wants to accomplish in the session. • Inquires about what issues would allow complete achievement of the goal. • Reflects heard issues back to the client. • Explores what must be resolved for the goal to be achieved.	4:30 Where would you like to start exploring all of the things you are bringing up here? Because you talk about confidence, you talk about trust; you talked about believing in your people. You talked about remembering that you have your own resources. Where do you think will be a good place?

COACHING COMPETENCY BEHAVIORAL MARKER	EVIDENCE OF MARKER
5. **Coach continues conversation in direction of client's desired outcome unless the client indicates otherwise.** • Recognizes emergence of new and/or competing session goal and recontracts as needed, as desired by client, the coaching session agreement and success measures.	*At no time did the client or the coach change direction or need to recontract.*

Competency 3: Creating Trust and Intimacy

COACHING COMPETENCY BEHAVIORAL MARKER	EVIDENCE OF MARKER
1. **Coach acknowledges and respects the client's work in the coaching process.** • Relates to the client through eye contact (for in-person or on-camera coaching); adapts to or matches the client's vocal rhythms; tracks with the client's language (body language or verbal language). • Understands, recognizes, and respects client's self-concept/ identity (the *who*). • Recognizes and affirms the client's courage and/or willingness to change.	*Though there is not specific language, the coach continuously asked the client's opinion and matched client's pace, rhythm, and energy.*

COACHING COMPETENCY BEHAVIORAL MARKER	EVIDENCE OF MARKER
2. Coach expresses support for the client. • (*Support* is not the same as *caretaking*.) • Makes empathic comments. • Expresses confidence in the client's capabilities. • Reflects the client's progress. • Acknowledges successes, strengths, and unique characteristics.	10:00 You sound like more confident, you said "be there," like in the way that it came out, it came out like with a confidence you were talking about. 28:00 Congratulations on your work.
3. Coach encourages and allows the client to fully express him/herself. • Uses silence that allows the client to process thinking and feeling. • Invites the client to disagree with the coach. • Affirmatively encourages the client to continue to express herself.	6:30 What is your hypothesis of what is going on there?

Competency 4: Coaching Presence

COACHING COMPETENCY BEHAVIORAL MARKER	EVIDENCE OF MARKER
1. **Coach acts in response to both the whole person of the client and what the client wants to accomplish in the session.** • "Whole person" includes, for example, when or how the client thinks, creates, and relates.	3:00 It is in the context within the last sessions of who you want to be as a leader.
2. **Coach is observant, empathetic and responsive.** • Treats the client's emotions respectfully, responsibly, and with unconditional positive regard.	10:00 You sound like more confident, you said "be there," like in the way that it came out, it came out like with a confidence you were talking about.
3. **Coach notices and explores energy shifts in the client.** • Shares observational feedback with the client when the client's vocal, verbal or body rhythms change.	10:00 Isn't the thing because in your voice different than before. You sound like more confident; you said "be there," like in the way that it came out, it came out like with a confidence you were talking about.
4. **Coach exhibits curiosity with the intent to learn more.** • Genuinely and authentically inquires about the client's agenda. • Genuinely and authentically inquires about aspects of the client as a person.	16:00 That voice was telling you to wait, where do you think it was coming from?

COACHING COMPETENCY BEHAVIORAL MARKER	EVIDENCE OF MARKER
5. Coach partners with the client by supporting the client to choose what happens in the session. • Extends an invitation to co-design or co-create session focus and direction. • Checks in on focus and direction during the session.	4:30 Where would you like to start exploring all of the things you are bringing up here? Because you talk about confidence, you talk about trust; you talked about believing in your people. You talked about remembering that you have your own resources. Where do you think will be a good place? 5:00 Okay, so inside of you, around what question would you like to answer or explore?
6. Coach partners with the client by inviting the client to respond in any way to the coach's contributions and accepts the client's response. • Partners with the client by, if offering assessments or opinions, doing so as an invitation for the client to use or not use, as she sees fit. • Hears and respects the client's frame of reference and thinking and, as appropriate, shares her own thinking and frame of reference without attachment.	21:00 What you're saying is it's about trusting people, is that it? 26:00 Just to make a comment, so when you're asking questions you said a couple of things that I wanted to bring to your attention. 27:30 I am asking you also if you want to consider as a possibility how you can use this not only for your work as a volunteer but also in your personal life.

COACHING COMPETENCY BEHAVIORAL MARKER	EVIDENCE OF MARKER
7. Coach partners with the client by playing back the client's expressed possibilities for the client to choose from. • Recognizes and reflects when, where, and with whom the client is at choice. • Paraphrases or clarifies coach's understanding of choices by the client.	4:30 Because you talk about confidence, you talk about trust; you talked about believing in your people. You talked about remembering that you have your own resources.
8. Coach partners with the client by encouraging the client to formulate his or her own learning. • Inquires about and/or champions the client's capability to assess her learning. • Inquires about the client's intuition and interpretation of the client's being, situation, and/or actions.	16:30 Okay so how do you think that this what you're saying affects your leadership? What happened when this was coming from your heart different than from your head? How does this affect what you are as a leader?

Competency 5: Active Listening

COACHING COMPETENCY BEHAVIORAL MARKER	EVIDENCE OF MARKER
1. Coach's questions and observations are customized by using what the coach has learned about whom the client is and the client's situation. • Listens to client processes, not only the specific meaning of client's language and concepts. • Uses what the client has said to form questions, not only about the situation but also about the client's being.	18:00 I heard in this conversation a couple of times where you had some realizations. One when you talk about discovering who you really are as a leader before people have figured out who you are like you knowing yourself.
2. Coach inquires about or explores the client's use of language. • Uses or incorporates the client's actual words into coach's paraphrasing, summarizing or questioning.	5:00 Okay, so inside of you, around what question would you like to answer or explore? 9:00 The lighthouse, I think. Or [foreign language] in Spanish, yeah. 9:30 So if you will be a lighthouse and you guide like in the middle for the boat how would that look like and how would you show up as a leader? 27:00 How is it in a nice way, in a very nice way how is it?
3. Coach inquires about or explores the client's emotions. • Asks about or reflects the client's emotions by recognizing mood, tone, affect, images or values.	*Missed opportunity*

COACHING COMPETENCY BEHAVIORAL MARKER	EVIDENCE OF MARKER
4. Coach inquires about or explores the client's tone of voice, pace of speech or inflection as appropriate. • Shares observational feedback when the client's vocal intonation or verbal pacing changes.	10:00 Isn't the thing because in your voice different than before. You sound like more confident; you said "be there," like in the way that it came out, it came out like with a confidence you were talking about.
5. Coach inquires about or explores the client's behaviors • Asks about the client's actions, reactions, or responses to people, places, or events.	16:30 How does this affect who you are as a leader?

COACHING COMPETENCY BEHAVIORAL MARKER	EVIDENCE OF MARKER
6. Coach inquires about or explores how the client perceives his/her world. • Asks about, identifies, or tests the client's beliefs, assumptions, values, and perspectives.	1:30 It seems that one of the talents is to remember that, is it? 3:00 Trusting you is also related to what you said before about being more confident as a leader. 6:30 What is your hypothesis of what is going on there? What do you think is coming, that need that people will think like you, do with you? 16:00 And that voice, sorry for interrupting you, but that voice was telling you to wait, where do you think it was coming from? 16:30 Okay so how do you think that this what you're saying affects your leadership? What happened when this was coming from your heart different than from your head? How does this affect who you are as a leader? 21:30 What you're saying is it's about trusting people, is that it? That you're trusting people even without seeing them.
7. When appropriate, coach is quiet and gives client time to think. • When listening to a response, coach gives sufficient time for the client to answer.	*During the entire session, the coach gave the client time to answer. This is hard to determine just from the transcript. A few examples are at 3:30, 5:00, 8:30, and 17:00.*

235

Competency 6: Powerful Questioning

COACHING COMPETENCY BEHAVIORAL MARKER	EVIDENCE OF MARKER
1. **Coach asks questions about the client; his/her way of thinking, assumptions, beliefs, values, needs, wants, etc.** • Inquires about thinking, assumptions, beliefs, and values without necessarily using those exact words in the coaching.	3:00 It is in the context within the last sessions of who you want to be as a leader. 6:30 What is your hypothesis of what is going on there? What do you think is coming, that need that people will think like you, do with you? 16:30 Okay so how do you think that this what you're saying affects your leadership? 16:30 How does this affect who you are as a leader?
2. **Coach's questions help the client explore beyond his/her current thinking to new or expanded ways of thinking about himself/herself.** • Questions and observations challenge the client's thinking. (Not in all sessions.) • Questions and observations move the client out of the current story she is telling and help her look forward.	8:00 Now that you realize that, now that you have the realization, who would you like to be in this situation as a leader? 9:30 So if you will be a lighthouse and you guide like in the middle for the boat how would that look like and how would you show up as a leader? 15:00 But what does this say about you? 16:00 And that voice, sorry for interrupting you, but that voice was telling you to wait, where do you think it was coming from?

COACHING COMPETENCY BEHAVIORAL MARKER	EVIDENCE OF MARKER
3. Coach's questions help the client explore beyond his/her current thinking to new or expanded ways of thinking about his/her situation. • Asks the client to look at the situation from different perspectives. • Asks questions that help the client reframe a problem or challenge to a more empowering frame for the client.	15:00 What do you think of this scene, if you put a little distance and you look at the scene like a helicopter perspective and you see that, you were talking before, what does this say about them?
4. Coach's questions help the client explore beyond current thinking towards the outcome s/he desires. • Asks the client to imagine/picture/articulate her desired future. • Questions help the client create new scenarios that would create success for her goal.	18:00 How can you apply these learnings to the question that we have today around building confidence, developing trust in yourself, and being the leader you want to be? 27:00 I am asking you also if you want to consider as a possibility how you can use this not only for your work as a volunteer but also in your personal life. How some conversations came up today about trust, confidence, control can be in some way showing up in other parts of your personal life that you cannot simply take advantage of.

COACHING COMPETENCY BEHAVIORAL MARKER	EVIDENCE OF MARKER
5. Coach asks clear, direct, primarily open-ended questions, one at a time, at a pace that allows for thinking and reflection by the client. • Asks questions that provoke inquiry—questions that cannot be answered literally with a yes or a no. • Allows the client to think before inserting another question.	20:30 And when you are less concerned about that, what is the consequence?
6. Coach's questions use the client's language and elements of the client's learning style and frame of reference. • Understands and works with the client's learning style (e.g., if client's preferred learning style is by doing, conceptualizing, experimenting, reflecting, visualizing, storytelling, etc.).	23:00 Going back to the metaphor that you used at the beginning of the lighthouse and when you talk about be there and what you're saying now about this trust, like trust and be there, trust in yourself in just being there, and knowing when to participate, not to participate, ready to trust in you, trust in your team how do you think that can translate into steps or actions, something you can do after this session?
7. Coach's questions are not leading, i.e. do not contain a conclusion or direction.	5.00 Okay, so inside of you, around what question would you like to answer or explore? 6:30 What is your hypothesis of what is going on there?

Competency 7: Direct Communication

COACHING COMPETENCY BEHAVIORAL MARKER	EVIDENCE OF MARKER
1. Coach shares observations, intuitions, comments, thoughts and feelings to serve the client's learning or forward movement. • Coach's statements help the client explore beyond her current thinking to new or expanded ways of thinking. • Coach's statements help the client explore beyond current thinking towards the outcome she desires.	7:00 Even this conversation is not in concrete! 18:00 I heard in this conversation a couple of times where you had some realizations. One when you talk about discovering who you really are as a leader before people have figured out who you are like you knowing yourself. The second one here about the learning about following your heart and from that the relationship and how that affect who you are a leader?
2. Coach shares observations, intuitions, comments, thoughts and feelings without any attachment to them being right. • Shares beliefs and assessments, not held as truths. • When sharing observations, intuition, comments, thoughts or feelings, coach clearly communicates that they are an "offer" for the client to respond to in any way she chooses.	18:00 I heard in this conversation a couple of times where you had some realizations. One when you talk about discovering who you really are as a leader before people have figured out who you are like you knowing yourself.

239

COACHING COMPETENCY BEHAVIORAL MARKER	EVIDENCE OF MARKER
3. Coach uses the client's language or language that reflects the client's way of speaking. • Uses the client's language as well as introducing new language. • Uses the client's words, speed, speech patterns, etc.	3:00 Trusting you is also related to what you said before about being more confident as a leader.
4. Coach's language is generally clear and concise. • When sharing observations, intuitions, comments, thoughts or feelings, coach clearly communicates and articulates in a manner that is easily and readily understood by the client.	3:00 It is in the context within the last sessions of who you want to be as a leader. 21:00 What you're saying is it's about trusting people. Is that it? That you're trusting people even without seeing them. 27:30 I am asking you also if you want to consider as a possibility how you can use this not only for your work as a volunteer but also in your personal life.
5. The coach allows the client to do most of the talking. • Talks considerably less than the client (in totality of conversation).	*During the session, the client did most of the talking. Specific examples in the transcript are at 1:00, 3:30, 5:30, 7:30, 8:30, 10:30–14:30, 18:30 and 23:30–25:30.*

COACHING COMPETENCY BEHAVIORAL MARKER	EVIDENCE OF MARKER
6. Coach allows the client to complete speaking without interrupting unless there is a stated coaching purpose to do so. • If the coach does not interrupt the client during the session, mark the marker. • If the coach interrupts on one or two occasions with a stated coaching purpose, mark the marker. • If the coach interrupts without a stated coaching purpose or interrupts frequently, do not mark the marker.	*The coach interrupted the client at 16:00. This interruption had a coaching purpose.* And that voice, sorry for interrupting you, but that voice was telling you to wait. Where do you think it was coming from? *Otherwise no interruptions were noted.*

Competency 8: Creating Awareness

COACHING COMPETENCY BEHAVIORAL MARKER	EVIDENCE OF MARKER
1. Coach invites client to state and/or explore his/her learning in the session about her/his situation (the what). • Asks about insights, learnings, and take-aways during and/or at end of session	22:00 Based on our conversation and what you wanted to accomplish in this session, where are you?

COACHING COMPETENCY BEHAVIORAL MARKER	EVIDENCE OF MARKER
2. Coach invites client to state and/or explore his/her learning in the session about her/himself (the who). • Inquires how new awareness/learning influences the client's behavior or way of being in the situation or perceiving herself.	9:30 So if you will be a lighthouse and you guide like in the middle for the boat how would that look like and how would you show up as a leader? 16:00 What happened when this was coming from your heart different than from your head? 20:30 And when you are less concerned about that, what is the consequence?
3. Coach shares what s/he is noticing about the client and/or the client's situation, and seeks the client's input or exploration. • As evidenced by coach inquiring about or noticing the client's emotions, body language, tone of voice, patterns of thought, and patterns of language.	18:00 I heard in this conversation a couple of times where you had some realizations. One when you talk about discovering who you really are as a leader before people have figured out who you are like you knowing yourself. The second one here about the learning about following your heart and from that the relationship and how that affect who you are a leader? How can you apply these learnings to the question that we have today around building confidence, developing trust in yourself, and being the leader you want to be?

COACHING COMPETENCY BEHAVIORAL MARKER	EVIDENCE OF MARKER
4. Coach invites client to consider how s/he will use new learning from the coaching. • States or links the client's new learning to the client's session or meta-goal, as a result of the coaching session process. • Invites the client to broaden the impact of learning to other situations or ways of being.	23:00 Going back to the metaphor that you used at the beginning of the lighthouse and when you talk about be there and what you're saying now about this trust, like trust and be there, trust in yourself in just being there, and knowing when to participate, not to participate, ready to trust in you, trust in your team how do you think that can translate into steps or actions, something you can do after this session?
5. Coach's questions, intuitions and observations have the potential to create new learning for the client. • Coach asks permission to consult, teach or mentor occasionally when in service of the client's immediate or longer-term agenda. • Coach's sharing of her own ideas, options, intuition or wisdom has the potential to expand the client's awareness and choice points or advance the client's agenda.	21:30 What you're saying is it's about trusting people, is that it? That you're trusting people even without seeing them. 17:30 I heard in this conversation a couple of times where you had some realizations. How can you apply these learnings to the question that we have today around building confidence?

Competencies 9, 10 and 11: Designing Actions, Planning and Goal Setting and Managing Progress and Accountability

COACHING COMPETENCY BEHAVIORAL MARKER	EVIDENCE OF MARKER
1. Coach invites or allows client to explore progress towards what s/he want to accomplish in the session. • Inquires about the client's progress toward the goal. • Follows up on the client's stated progress, or lack of progress, toward the goal.	22:00 We need to start wrapping up. Based on our conversation and what you wanted to accomplish in this session, where are you?
2. Coach assists the client to design what actions/thinking client will do after the session in order for the client to continue moving toward the client's desired outcomes. • Actions may look like: further thinking; additional feeling or living with an idea; self-inquiry; behavior change; task completion; research; or experimentation.	23:30 How do you think that can translate into steps or actions, something you can do after this session?

COACHING COMPETENCY BEHAVIORAL MARKER	EVIDENCE OF MARKER
3. Coach invites or allows client to consider her/his path forward, including, as appropriate, support mechanisms, resources and potential barriers. • Explores likelihood of an action to occur in the future (e.g. use of a scaling question). • Inquires about the client's feeling about the action. • Tests the client's level of willingness to execute.	18:00 I heard in this conversation a couple of times where you had some realizations. One when you talk about discovering who you really are as a leader before people have figured out who you are like you knowing yourself. The second one here about the learning about following your heart and from that the relationship and how that affect who you are a leader? How can you apply these learnings to the question that we have today around building confidence, developing trust in yourself, and being the leader you want to be?
4. Coach assists the client to design the best methods of accountability for her/himself. • Coach can serve as an accountability partner on occasion. • Inquires about other forms of support for client accountability structures.	*Not demonstrated*
5. Coach partners with the client to close the session. • Invites the client to consider how she wants to complete the session. • Checks in with the client on what topics the client is complete with and what.	26:30 Okay, how do you want to wrap up this session today?

COACHING COMPETENCY BEHAVIORAL MARKER	EVIDENCE OF MARKER
6. Coach notices and reflects client's progress. • Celebrates the client's success when the client executes on agreed action commitments. • Inquires about obstacles that got in the way of the client's efforts to follow through on actions.	26:00 Just to make a comment, so when you're asking questions you said a couple of things that I wanted to bring to your attention. When you ask questions and when you're working with people and delegating activities you see you're going to be trusting them. So it seems that you may bring consciously your belief that they can be trusted and you are choosing to trust them. And at the same time you are going to support them so I want to be supportive I want to be able to think I will be there and at the same time be more comfortable in delegating tasks to other people.

ACKNOWLEDGMENTS

DAMIAN GOLDVARG:

I would like to thank all my teachers and colleagues who inspire me to learn, grow, and develop. I would like to recognize all the participants who have attended our coaching, mentor coaching, and coaching supervision certification programs worldwide for the last eight years. They've inspired me to keep working on developing high standards for our professional coaching practice. I would also like to thank ICF staff for the incredible work they do to develop coaching worldwide, in particular Magda Mook and George Rogers. Finally, I would like to thank the coaches who were involved in supporting this book, including Jeff Auerbach for editing and publishing the book and my co-writers Pat Mathews and Norma Perel, my mother.

NORMA PEREL:

I want to thank Damian and Pat for collaborating in writing the book. The foundation of the book was the original book written in Spanish on coaching competencies that I co-authored with Damian. I thank all the great masters from whom I learned so much. I want to thank Damian who has always been a source of inspiration for me and given me the opportunity to share the writing of this book, and Ariel, my other son. Both supported the continuation of an endless transformational learning both professionally and personally.

PAT MATHEWS:

The completion of this book would not have been possible without the support of so many. To Magda Mook, George Rogers and Janet Harvey for selecting me for the first meeting that led to the formation of the coaching competency behavioral markers. I haven't always cheered about that day, but it was critical to the writing of this book. To Margaret Krigbaum, Soren Holm and Hope Langner—my partners on the core team for the development of the markers. Those many virtual meetings and face-to-face marathons were both hard and rewarding. To Julie Shows, my partner at Georgetown and in so many of the markers trainings—your friendship and unwavering confidence in me has made me a better person. To my faculty colleagues and assessors at Georgetown—your initial "impressive resistance" to the pilot markers training and subsequent powerful learning and partnering has made me a better coach, teacher, and supporter of the assessment process. To all friends, coaching colleagues, clients, and others who shared their support in one way or another, you will never be forgotten. Many thanks.

ABOUT THE AUTHORS

DAMIAN GOLDVARG, PH.D., MCC

Damian Goldvarg has thirty years of experience in providing leadership development services including: executive assessment and coaching, facilitation, leadership training, strategic planning, and team building. Originally from Argentina, he has worked with individuals and organizations in over fifty countries, including the Americas, Europe, Africa, and Asia, offering services in English, Spanish, and Portuguese.

He is a Master Certified Coach and received his Ph.D. in Organizational Psychology from Alliant University in California. He is an accredited coach supervisor (ESIA) and facilitates certifications in professional coaching, mentor coaching, and coaching supervision. He was the 2013-2014 ICF global president.

Dr. Goldvarg's work with multinational Fortune 100 companies, governments, and community-based organizations focuses on enhancing productivity, communication, and leadership capacity to improve the quality of the work, and well-being, of those individuals he coaches.

Damian is the author of five coaching books, four of them in Spanish. He has also been awarded the Circle of Distinction by the ICF for significant contribution to the field of coaching. His website is www.goldvargconsulting.com.

PATRICIA A. MATHEWS, RN, MA, MCC

Patricia Mathews, Master Certified Coach, is the owner of Mathews Associates, a leadership and executive coaching business. She completed the Georgetown Leadership Coaching Certificate Program in 2001 and has done extensive work in mentor coaching both within the Georgetown Program and with coaches who are working toward an ICF credential. Pat received her MCC from the International Coach Federation in 2006.

Pat chaired the ICF Credentialing and Accreditation committee for two years and served on the committee for four years. She served on the ICF global board of directors for five years and served as vice chair in 2016.

Pat has been a volunteer on the ICF PCC/MCC Assessors Team for 10 years. She was one of the members of the core team that developed the behavioral markers for ICF. She delivered the training for the trainers in this process. She has delivered the markers training for both ICF and the Georgetown Leadership Coaching Certificate Program.

Since 2006, she has been on the faculty of the Georgetown Leadership Coaching Certificate Program and served as a program director from 2010 to 2014.

Pat lives with her husband in Philadelphia, Pennsylvania, West Palm Beach, Florida, and Harvey Cedars, New Jersey. She is an avid walker, average tennis player, and enjoys traveling with her husband, Norm. They have traveled extensively to all seven continents and have taken two six-month world cruises. She loves the beach and recharges there, as well as enjoys time spent there with her friends. She is the mom of two sons, both of whom live in Massachusetts. Her website is www.patmathews.com.

NORMA PEREL, MS, MCC

Norma Perel is a Master Certified Coach by the International Coach Federation. She holds a degree in Psychology from the University of Buenos Aires. She was certified as a coach at the Argentina School of NLP & Coaching, where she served as supervisor, evaluator and mentor coach. She is a mentor coach, certified supervisor and NLP practitioner. She is a founding member and former board member of the ICF Argentina Chapter. She was the director of Continuing Coaching Education and ambassador of Continuing Coaching Education for Latin America. She is a member of the Goldvarg Consulting Group staff. She co-facilitates, with Damián Goldvarg, virtual groups for certification in mentor coaching for Latin America and Spain. She collaborated with Damián Goldvarg authoring two books: *Applied Coaching Competencies* and *Mentor Coaching in Action*. With other colleagues she co-authored the book: *Coaching. A World of Possibilities*.

ABOUT THE EXECUTIVE EDITOR

JEFFREY E. AUERBACH, PH.D, MCC

J effrey Auerbach served on the International Coach Federation global board of directors and held the office of vice president. He also served as both president, and as an international board member of the Association of Coach Training Organizations, an organization that has had a long strategic relationship with the International Coach Federation, for five years. He has served on the ICF Governance Workgroup, and also on the editorial board of coaching: *International Journal of Theory, Research and Practice.* An expert on emotional intelligence in the workplace, Dr. Auerbach is a frequent speaker at academic and professional conferences on positive psychology, well-being and emotional intelligence.

Auerbach is the author of the best-selling book, *Personal and Executive Coaching; The Well-Being Coaching Workbook; Seeing the Light: What Organizations Need to Know—The State of the Coaching Industry Report,* and the editor of *Building Competence in Personal and Executive Coaching.* He is the co-author, with Dr. Sandra Foster from Stanford University, of *Positive Psychology in Coaching: Applying Science to Executive and Personal Coaching.* Auerbach is the founder and president of College of Executive Coaching. His website is www.executivecoachcollege.com.